SUPERBOWL

SUPERBOWL

BRYAN BRETT

WARD LOCK LIMITED · LONDON
IN ASSOCIATION WITH GRANADA TELEVISION

First published in Great Britain in 1986
by Ward Lock Limited, 8 Clifford Street,
London W1X 1RB, an Egmont Company

Designed by Angela King
Text set in Garamond
by M & R Computerised Typesetting Ltd., Grimsby.
Printed in England by James Upton Ltd Birmingham and London

Front cover Top left *Tony Allcock, a hot favourite for* Superbowl *Champion 1986.* Top right *David Bryant, 1984 winner and 1985 runner-up in* Superbowl. Below *David Bryant and Noel Burrows during the 1985* Superbowl *final.*
Title page *Stage One: a capacity audience enjoyed the 1985* Superbowl *final between Bryant and Burrows.*
Back cover *The* Superbowl *trophy.*

The photographs on page 14 were reproduced by the kind permission of the author.

British Library Cataloguing in Publication Data

Brett, Bryan
    Superbowl.
    1. Bowling on the green
    I. Title
    796.31 GV909

ISBN 0-7063-6495-3

CONTENTS

SUPERBOWL

A positive approach from John Bell.

Left to right *Paul Doherty with Bryan Brett and Jimmy Davidson outside Stage One.*

October 1984, saw a revolution in bowls. It took place in the unusual setting of a television studio in the city centre of Manchester and brought together the ancient, and very different, worlds of flat and crown green bowls. Two games which had been keeping a low profile through many centuries were suddenly given an injection of show-business razzmatazz. It was enough to sweep away the traditional dogmacy that had kept bowls stagnating in complacency for so many years.

'*Superbowl*', said its creator, Granada's Head of Sport Paul Doherty, 'is the biggest thing to happen in bowls since Francis Drake enjoyed his famous game and then attended to the Spanish Armada.' The title of *Superbowl* emerged naturally as the competition took shape. The competition was immediately appealing to the flat green players and gave the crown green bowlers a rare chance to pit their wits and their own particular skills against the other code. 'We wanted a super competition and we were playing bowls. *Superbowl* seemed to be the obvious title', said Doherty, who first discovered the potential in bringing the two codes together from Granada's involvement in crown green competitions.

The venue for *Superbowl* is a television studio — Granada's multi-purpose Stage One — that has housed several productions, ranging from comedies to scenes from the major drama series, J. B. Priestley's *Lost Empires*. Creating an arena for *Superbowl* made special demands on the imagination of Granada's Head of Design, Roy Stonehouse. He responded by providing a setting that was impressive, comfortable for spectators, and functional to meet television production requirements. 'The audience is an integral part of bowls and to create the right atmosphere we designed the arena on the lines of the Coliseum', explained Doherty. Banks of spectators either side of the rink achieved exactly the right effect. The atmosphere generated throughout also owed much to the audience who were predominantly crown green orientated, and quick to show appreciation and offer advice — whether required or not.

If the setting was impressive, then the quality of player matched it. Granada went for the best from both sides and they got it — flat green champions and leading crown players. From the start, Doherty insisted on a strong representation of women players, so six places in the field of thirty-two were reserved for women in the initial year. This was to be increased to eight in the following year. He explains:

I am a firm believer in encouraging sports where women can compete on equal lines. Bowls officials were reluctant in the first place to agree but we stuck to our guns and they came round to our way of thinking. The risk area was bringing together the flat and the crown players, as we knew there would not be an equal standard. But we were also aware that the crown players would make rapid improvements in playing flat when they lost their normal cavalier approach.

The cavalier approach was very evident in the first *Superbowl* where the crown players delighted the Stage One and television audiences, but generally made little impression on the flat green players, who soon made themselves at home on the rink. The main difference between the two games is that the crown green players use bowls that are much lighter than those in flat green bowling. They also play on greens that have a pronounced crown.

The planning for the inaugural *Superbowl* started around an office desk in Granada's sprawling complex in Manchester and the response was so encouraging that Doherty was soon able to bounce his revolutionary ideas off a number of leading crown green personalities. They included Manchester City Secretary, Bernard Halford, a man who has played bowls at top level and who has been lobbying for greater television involvement for years. Greater Manchester's top crown green official, Eric Rhodes, was asked to lend his weight and, eventually, he took over the organizing of stewards and many other background duties. 'A dear friend', are the words Doherty uses to describe the considerable contribution Eric Rhodes made before he sadly died a few months after the second *Superbowl.*

My role, in those early, exciting days, was to make the first approach to the British and World Indoor Bowling Councils. Their immediate response was one of some caution and I was left with the distinct impression that the flat green world was not too enthralled with the idea of having a competition of such enormity thrust into their already crowded programme. However, such was Doherty's enthusiasm that he would not consider anything short of approval from the right authorities; and, with the support of Martin Conlin (Secretary, British Isles Indoor Bowls Council) and Jimmy Davidson (Secretary, World Bowls Council) agreement was reached in July, 1984 — barely three months before the competition was to begin.

Three months earlier, Doherty had taken his idea to Granada's Managing Director, David Plowright, and Programme Controller, Mike Scott. 'Unlike many conversations about televised live action, this was not a hopeful search for the next visual activity to match the success story of snooker on the small screen;' recalls Doherty, 'it was a discussion with a sharp focus.' The game of bowls had been high on the agenda for some time. Three years before *Superbowl,* Granada had made a big investment in coverage of a three-day crown green event, the Bass Masters, and this was followed by the Greenall County Classic, both of which are now well-established in the calendar. Plowright, a firm believer in bowls, gave Doherty the support to establish with *Superbowl* not only a first for television but also a first use for Stage One, a building on a large expanse of derelict land which replaced the film studio that was burned down in January, 1983, during the making of *The Jewel in the Crown,* the internationally acclaimed series. Indoor bowling was one of the sports included in the planning of Stage One.

The first *Superbowl* did not attract network interest, despite the competition including the best of the flat and crown green bowling worlds. Granada were a major company alone with their £250,000 investment, although Yorkshire and Scotland did take some interest and the minor Border company took all the transmissions. So the network missed a slice of bowling history, and compelling television, as David Bryant, the biggest name in the game, took on the Cumbrian John Bell in an epic Saturday-night final that lasted two and a half hours. It was an event which kept the audience in Stage One — and those viewing at home — on the edge of their seats. It started with live cover on Granada at 10.35 p.m., and continued through three titanic sets until Bryant elected to go for a long lead which was to make the world's leading player an appropriate winner of the first *Superbowl* title (and the record £10,000 first prize). His opponent, Bell, ran his final bowl of the match into one of his own bowls leaving Bryant a relieved and delighted winner by 5–7, 7–5, 7–6 at 1.11 a.m. on Sunday, 21 October.

Scoring is based on a player counting one shot for every bowl he gets closer to the jack than his opponent. As both players have four bowls each, it is possible to count a maximum of four shots at one end. The *Superbowl* game is based on sets of 7–up (i.e. seven points up), so it is, in theory, possible to win a set in two ends. The sets system may have been controversial with the establishment, but it proved to be highly successful from a spectator's point of view. It was the insistence of national bowling coach Jimmy Davidson which virtually forced the acceptance of the sets system which has, naturally, delighted the television executives searching for thrills in their sport. The action was instant, and the excitement was kept to fever pitch throughout the six days of *Superbowl*. Audience reaction from the opening day had been encouraging and the 1,000-seat Stage One studio was regularly packed. For the second year, capacity was increased by two hundred seats but this was not enough to satisfy a bowling audience whose appetite for indoor bowls had been sharpened by *Superbowl*. More than 12,000 spectators were to be packed in for the eleven sessions of the second *Superbowl*. 'All tickets went within four days and I regret that we cannot expand the walls of Stage One to increase the capacity', aplogized Doherty, to the thousands of addicts who were disappointed. He predicted that thirty-five million viewers would watch *Superbowl* in its second year, once the whole network took the event. It became the first nationally televised six-day bowling event to appear on Independent Television. Granada's research department came up with some fascinating facts. A total of three and a half million adults watched the 1984 *Superbowl*, or part of it, from an adult audience in Granada's region of over five million. The average adult audience numbered 641,000 and the peak viewing figure for one show was 886,000 homes. This figure was recorded during the games between Norma Shaw and Ken Strutt, and Jim Baker against Len Higginbottom.

After existing as an invitation event in its first year, the competition saw some changes with regard to how the flat green authorities decided on their representatives for *Superbowl* number two. The British Isles Indoor Bowls Council insisted that the champions from Scotland, England, Wales and Northern Ireland, and the British Isles title winner should get automatic entry. The four semi-finalists from 1984 *Superbowl* were also to be asked back and each of the four flat green governing bodies were asked to nominate a player. The British Isles Women's Indoor Bowls Council proposed a representative from Wales, Ireland and Scotland to join Norma Shaw in the flat section of sixteen players.

Choosing representatives on the crown side remained on invitation basis, with the emphasis clearly on the top players from their own particular version of bowls who would be able to adjust to the demands of the flat. Only one crown man, Noel Burrows, reached the quarter-finals in the first year, and his performance was a tantalizing taste of what was to come in *Superbowl* two.

Noel Burrows, the pride of the crown green world and a particular favourite of the Stage One audience, started his bid on the second morning of the 1984

Over 12,000 spectators were packed into Stage One for the eleven sessions of Superbowl 1985.

David Bryant entering into the spirit of the competition.

Burrows and Bryant take a closer look at the Superbowl *trophy.*

competition and delighted his fans with a 7–6, 7–3 win over Michael Dunlop, the Belfast player who was then the British Isles Indoor Singles Champion. Burrows followed that by beating Karen Galvin, the brightest of the young crown lady players, 7–5, 7–0 to secure a quarter-final place against John Bell, a determined yet very approachable man who had turned to bowls after an injury stopped him playing rugby at county standard in 1975. Bell's greater experience of the rink game finally came through, but only after Burrows had taken a set off him on a Thursday afternoon that drew a near-capacity audience to Stage One. The sets went 7–4, 4–7 and 7–3 in Bell's favour, but experts from both codes had seen enough to realize that the gap between the top flat and crown men was closing.

In Burrows' case the gap disappeared the following year when he stormed through to the final beating four flat green players on the way. His was the toughest draw; even the hot favourite Bryant had what looked to be an easier task with only two crown green players to beat on his route to the final. The appearance of Burrows on the second morning of the 1985 *Superbowl* again pulled in the fans, many from his big crown green following. He did not disappoint them, opening with a two sets to one victory over the outstanding young Northern Ireland player Rodney McCutcheon. He followed that by dropping a first set (6–7) to the Welsh Outdoor Lady Champion, Julie Davies, but then came back strongly to win the second (7–3) and then the third, on a desperate measure, 7–6. Frank McCartney, the National Indoors Singles Champion, waited for Burrows in the quarter-finals but, despite a rally in the second set, was to go out 7–2, 7–6. Willie Wood, a semi-finalist in the first year and a player of enormous talent, had picked his bowls carefully for the 1985 event. They served him well and he was almost unbeatable on certain shorter marks, but Burrows matched him well. Wood took the first set 7–5 and if the crown green supporters sagged, Burrows did not. He had enough experience from the hard world of crown green bowls to call on and by now was also good enough to earn flat green trials for England. He seized the initiative and started to nag away at Wood's confidence to win the second set by a resounding 7–1. Burrows added an impressive 7–4 last set win to clinch a final appearance that virtually every knowledgeable follower of the game of bowls had believed was out of his reach for some time.

Bryant, always a firm favourite to repeat his 1984 success, had picked his way through the top half of the draw, experiencing discomfort against a couple of resolute characters from the crown green world: Mick Robinson, a left-hander from Dewsbury with an awkward delivery style; and former professional bowler Norman Fletcher. Robinson almost upset Bryant in an opening set that went the distance, with the favourite winning 7–6. The crab-like, back-of-the-hand style of delivery used by the twenty-eight-year-old Robinson was, in a way, reminiscent of Bryant and his precision play certainly had echoes of the great man about it. Bryant tied it up 7–4 in the second set for a win that was at no point easy.

If he was glad to see the back of one crown green player, Bryant was about to see much more of another in the dogged Fletcher. A huge audience turned up for this clash, late on the Wednesday evening. The match had the smell of drama about it as soon as it was made, although the likelihood of Fletcher winning was something nobody could genuinely anticipate. That did not stop the followers of the publican from Leigh in Lancashire giving the occasion all the emotion of an old-time battle from the great days of professional bowling. Fletcher froze in the first set, being whitewashed and trying to play the game in a way that really is foreign to his fighting nature. With the second set came a different Fletcher — a determined, fiery character with the gloves off. 'If I can't beat them, I'll strike them off', he had promised in his plan to knock the Bryant machine out of gear.

Fletcher, the deadliest of strikers from the crown green, set about Bryant, often contravening the laws of the flat game and upsetting the purists. He walked up the rink when he should have stood still, strolled back to the mat when he should have been at the head and even pleaded ignorance of the rules. Those who know him accept that flat green laws are something Fletcher may pick up in time, particularly as he rarely plays the game and believes so much in his natural ability as a bowler that he simply turns up on the day, without preparation, to take on the world's top exponent. But the roof of Stage One almost came off on the night that Fletcher took the second set 7–5 and was, suddenly, a player who demanded respect from the best. Roared on by a crowd strongly in his favour, Fletcher pushed Bryant hard in the final set before losing 7–5. It was a night when Fletcher probably decided that there was much more to this rink game than he had believed, and one on which Bryant's reputation soared in the estimation of the crown green world for the way he put up with, and finally conquered, antics he will probably never encounter again.

Jim Boyle, twice Scottish Indoor Champion, was Bryant's next opponent and he had already made his mark. He opened the competition with a seven ends win over Nancy Gibson, a former National Champion from Belfast, to set a hot pace in the race for the £1,000 for the fastest finish. It was a pace nobody could beat and Boyle received his £1,000 from Ken Wilkinson, Chairman of Liverpool Victoria Insurance Company, who had arrived on the scene to pull off a sponsorship *coup* by backing *Superbowl*. Boyle, having toppled the fancied Tony Allcock in the second round, found Bryant in top form in the quarter-finals and went out in straight sets. He had been in trouble against National Singles Champion, Allcock, losing the first set 7–2 before winning the second two 7–2, 7–4. At least the defeat allowed Allcock to take his place on the commentary team.

Commentary during the 1984 *Superbowl* had been in the hands of the vastly experienced John Freeman and Hugh Johns, supported by Director of Coaching, Jimmy Davidson, David Bryant and myself. John Freeman, the man who hosted the *Face to Face* series, had the experience of 750 on-screen appearances (none relating to bowls) and his passion for the sport was such that he jumped at the chance of commentating at *Superbowl*, but overseas commitments robbed us of his services in the second year. Hugh Johns, commentator and presenter for twenty years, had switched from soccer — where he had covered four World Cup Finals — to bowls, with enormous success. He already had extensive knowledge of the game, much of it as a result of his wife Joan's involvement as Secretary of the Welsh Ladies Indoor Bowling Association.

The player who thrilled us all and won the hearts of the spectators more than any other was the Scottish housewife, Jeanette Conlan. She came to *Superbowl* as the Scottish and British Isles Ladies Champion with a preference for indoor bowls, as she declared herself 'a fair weather player' outdoors. Jeanette could have gone out in her game when a vital rub went against the crown green's Len Higginbottom. The Scottish woman won that cliff-hanger two sets to one and found herself facing a man from the West Country, David Cutler, who was rated as the most consistent outdoor singles player in England. On the *Superbowl* rink, reputations counted for nothing as the inspired Jeanette recovered from losing the first set 7–6 to win the next two 7–5 and 7–6. She was allowed little chance of repeating that sort of treatment in the quarter-finals with the Irish Champion and former World Champion, Jim Baker, as her opponent. The odds were heavily against Jeanette and there was increasing support for Baker who had started as second favourite. But Baker was to become another scalp claimed by the Scottish housewife with a sensational 7–3, 7–5 scoreline that clinched a semi-final appearance against Bryant. This occasion finally proved to be too much for Jeanette. Bryant was in formidable form and immediately stamped his authority on the game with a 7–0 opening set. He added a 7–2 second set victory that ended a dream for Jeanette but sent her back to her Dalkeith home having thoroughly enjoyed her week and helped justify the decision to include leading ladies in *Superbowl*.

The Bryant versus Burrows final, in the second *Superbowl,* crystallized the event's original concept. Here was the world of flat green's top player competing against the crown green bowler who had won everything in his own version of the game, and was ready to bridge the gap by stepping into flat green bowling. Stage One was packed; spectators crammed into the overflow commentary position, hospitality boxes and any spot that offered a glimpse of the historic confrontation. Those who could not get into the 'Coliseum' had to be content with viewing on additional television monitors that were set up in the foyer. The final was also going out during I.T.V.'s new two-hour Saturday afternoon sports programme, on a delayed tape because of scheduling. Viewing figures for that programme were to establish bowls second only to snooker in appeal at that time. In 1986 the final is to be shown live on the network on Saturday evening and into Sunday morning, if an over-run is needed. This is the format that has captivated the viewers and the Stage One audience.

Burrows, wearing the light blue of his favourite Manchester City soccer team, opened confidently, winning the first two ends. Bryant threatened to turn the opening set, however, with a three off the sixth end for a 5–3 lead. He added another single and Burrows faced set point. He responded with two doubles, split by a dead end, to take the first set. Bryant led briefly at the start of the second set, before a couple of doubles gave Burrows a 4–1 advantage. Burrows then conceded a couple of chalks before picking up another double and was on the way to a 7–5 second set success that had the spectators in uproar. They were immediately silenced as Bryant hit back with a double, treble and another double to take the third set 7–0, with Burrows appearing to take a breather. Bryant's title soon began to slip, however. He led just once in the fourth set, at 2–1. This was followed by five points from four ends — Bryant replied with a double — giving Burrows a 6–4 lead, only a point away from a staggering success. Bryant refused to concede and levelled at 6–6. The next end was to be the final one; with Bryant unable to beat the shot bowl of Burrows. Twice he failed by centimetres leaving Burrows *Superbowl* Champion of 1985, and richer by £10,000.

Burrow's performance had given new impetus to a bowls revolution that was taking place in the traditional crown green areas. Noel Burrows came to *Superbowl* 1985, not to be an extra making up the cast, but to be the star, and he was exactly that.

HISTORY OF BOWLS

In the nineteenth century many public houses had their own bowling greens. Here regular crown green players at the Spread Eagle, near Blackburn, Lancashire, pose for a group photograph.

Bernard Kelly, of Hyde, collects the Waterloo Handicap trophy in October 1954 to become the only player to win the leading crown green event in successive years.

How did the game of bowls begin and develop? References to bowls in classical works over the centuries, establish it as having ancient roots. The game can be traced back to Asia Minor, and to the ancient kingdom of Lydia, where it was a popular form of relaxation for five or six centuries before the birth of Christ. In those days stones were used; they were thrown, or bowled, towards a mark. The Latin term *Jactus Lapidum* — casting of stone — is believed to have led to the word 'jack' being used to describe the smaller bowl which sets a mark. Bowls is thought to have come to Britain *via* France during the Norman Conquest and was either bowling to a set object or bowling to a pre-drawn circle with the intention of knocking out other bowls.

The popularity of bowls during the Middle Ages was such that the game was banned following pressure from King Edward III and Richard II on the grounds that it interfered with archery practice. Shakespeare makes reference to bowls in *Richard II*: 'Twill make me think the world is full of rubs and that my fortune runs against the bias', ponders Queen Isobel in answer to a suggestion that she should play bowls with a Lady-in-waiting. In 1541, the playing of bowls was still frowned upon. Later, an act of parliament decreed that apprentices and labourers were only to play at Christmas unless they had permission from their masters. Even if they did gain this permission, games had to be played on their masters' greens. The penalty for playing on other greens was a fine of 6s. 8d. This act lingered on and was in force until 1845. In the Middle Ages, private greens were limited to people who owned land with an annual value of £100 or more and they had to be licensed by the local authority. These restrictions were lifted in 1555. Even in the nineteenth century, the game was banned because of connections with pothouses (pubs). However, respectability was obtained when Scottish enthusiasts drafted an acceptable form of rules in 1849. In England, the flat version of the game started to get organized in the late nineteenth century, thanks to the establishment of the London and Southern Counties and the Midlands Counties Associations. The English Bowling Association followed in 1903. Prominent in the development of bowls was a sporting figure normally associated with cricket, W. G. Grace, who was the first President of the English Bowling Association. He played in the first international series of bowls matches between the home counties in 1903, and helped to draw up rules for the International Bowling Board. Grace also suggested that an indoor practise mat used by cricketers would be suitable for bowls.

The biased (or weighted) bowl of the sixteenth century had a hole drilled into one side in which a weight was inserted. Later, this was abandoned in favour of designing the bowl's running sole into a shape that would have the same effect.

Before 1871, the comparative testing of bowls was unknown and, as they were hand-made and finished, it was impossible to match them perfectly. However, in 1871, the Glasgow bowls-maker, Thomas Taylor, constructed the first testing table and enabled accurate comparative tests to be made. He produced a range of five bowls, each with a different bias. A few years later, the Scottish Bowling

Association carried out a number of tests and, in 1893, adopted the number three bias as the one that had achieved the required standard. This was eventually adopted by the flat green bowling world. The date on which the standardization of the crown green jack occurred has not been recorded. (The crown green jack is biased unlike the flat jack.) They decided that a number two bias was too weak and the number three, too strong. They asked for the number two to be strengthened and the two full bias standard jack was adopted.

In crown green bowling, the height of a green's crown is a recommended 30 cm (12 in). This is the difference, on grass, between the two codes of bowls although, until the arrival of *Superbowl,* they were miles apart. *Superbowl* has brought together the two games in a way which few would have thought possible in view of their vastly different characteristics. The crown green game is restricted to an area stretching from the Midlands up to Yorkshire, Cumbria, Lancashire, North Wales and across to the Isle of Man. There are other outposts, notably on the south coast where Bournemouth boasts a public crown green. Abroad, there is one crown green in Tulsa in the American Mid-West.

Records show that the crown green game was being enjoyed in the eighteenth and nineteenth centuries. The Bowling Green, a public house in Manchester a few miles from the city centre traces the origins of its green back to the mid-seventeenth century. But it was about a century ago that the game really started to get organized. Lancashire formed an association for counties in 1888 and this led to the creation of the Crown Green Association (now the British Crown Green Association) in 1907. The British Parks Association was established in 1911, three years after the creation of the Lancashire Professional Bowling Association (now the British P.B.A.), a body designed to look after the interests of players who competed for cash prizes and were not amateurs.

The existence of crown greens in the seaside resort of Blackpool can be traced back to 1788. Yet it was nearly one hundred years later in 1873 that the first of the town's famous competitions, the Talbot Tournament, was introduced. The Talbot ran for more than a hundred years and was sadly abandoned, because of losses, in 1975. Noel Burrows, the 1985 *Superbowl* Champion, played on the finals day of the last Talbot. Another *Superbowl* competitor, Arthur Murray, reached the semi-finals on that day. The departure of the Talbot left the way clear for its big rival, the Waterloo Handicap which was run in the same town and became established as the leading crown green competition. The competition started in 1907 with 320 entries. Today, it has 2,048 entries with many more bowlers turning up during the six-week staging of the competition in the hope of getting a place as a reserve. Tickets for the Waterloo finals are snapped up, by written application only, nearly eight months before the big day. The stadium accommodates 4,000 people on stands and terraces which surround the most famous turf in the crown green game. Arthur Murray holds a special place in the history of the Waterloo. He is the only player still competing to have won the event twice, first in 1973, and again in 1978. Bernard Kelly of Hyde won the title in 1953 and 1954 but retired soon after on health grounds.

The biggest prize in crown green bowling is £5,500 which is awarded to the winner of the Bass Masters Classic, an event covered by Granada and totalling £10,000 in prize money.

These days, crown green rules come under the British Crown Green

Association banner. The only exception is the professional panel that still operates on a daily basis around the Bolton area which decrees that two throws of the jack are allowed. Normally, only one throw of the jack is permitted and this ruling extends to the Waterloo Handicap (which used to play under its own Waterloo rules). These include the cutting of straws to decide an end instead of taking a measure. The player who could cut the shortest straw and balance it on the jack and his nearest bowl was the winner, so a steady hand was required.

The 1913 Waterloo Final was historic in that the two contestants were brothers — Gerrard and Richard Hart. Gerrard, a professional, was the winner. Play continued throughout World War I and entries reached a peak in 1919 when there were 1,228 competitors. In 1921, Lancashire's professionals were banned by their Association because of a dispute over advertising gambling. Gerrard Hart ignored the ban to play, and he beat Sir Lindsay Parkinson, founder of the famous building firm, in the opening round, 21–17. Tom Richardson, from Blackpool's south shore area, carved his own *niche* in the Waterloo records when he recorded a hat-trick of losing final appearances. Richardson reached the last sixteen in 1948, the year the loudspeaker equipment was first used, at the age of sixty-seven. The 1949 Waterloo was won by Joe Egan with a pair of bowls he had bought for five shillings in a Southport salesroom twenty years earlier. Bernard Kelly's bowls in 1953 and 1954 cost him twenty-five shillings and he remains the only man to have won the event in successive years. Jim Collen's 1975 record of winning the Waterloo, and then the Champion of Champions title a few days later on the same green, was equalled by Cheshire's Stan Frith who won both events in 1984, a year in which he also captured the All-England title — an astonishing feat.

Manchester was also a favourite for crown green bowling in the late nineteenth and early twentieth centuries. Top players went under assumed names to try to confuse gamblers and get their odds increased. Games of 101-up (101 points), lasting a day, were commonplace with William 'Toss' Taylor of Little Hulton, just one of the players with the stamina to survive that sort of ordeal. He won a game at the Golden Lion, a mile from Manchester city centre, by 81–70, in June 1894, against a player known only as 'Jitter'. Taylor went on to win the 1906 Talbot Tournament and became so good that he had to concede starts of 15 to his opponents in games of 81-up. Today's players are generally accustomed to games of 21-up, although there are still a number of handicaps offering 31-up and 41-up matches. Prize money has kept pace with increasing interest and, with sponsorship playing a bigger part, there are a number of competitions offering winning prizes of between £1,000 and £2,000. These are within reach for an entry fee of only a few pounds.

Each of the fifteen county areas competes for the Crosfield Cup (which is the British County Championship), first in groups and then on a straight knock-out basis. These teams include all the crown green players who have taken part in *Superbowl*. A county appearance is still regarded as an honour because the financial rewards go to the counties rather than to individuals.

PLAYERS – MEN

David Bryant in action.

Brian Duncan, rated the top crown player, takes on John Bell.

The massive shadow of David Bryant seemed to put everybody else in the shade when the names of players to appear in the first *Superbowl* were known. The game's number one player lived up to his reputation; he won the first title and was runner-up to Noel Burrows in the second. He started as a 5–2 favourite — the odds were the same when the second year started — and there was plenty of support for a man rarely seen in the north-west of England.

Bryant's first appearance on *Superbowl* helped to bring a full house to Stage One. The game's greatest ever player faced an opponent in Arthur Murray who was the only crown man still playing to have won the famous Waterloo Handicap twice. Murray was also an enthusiastic convert to the flat code, having joined the Swinton Club shortly before the first *Superbowl*. However, that sort of crown pedigree and limited flat experience was not enough to cause Bryant any problems. The game ended in straight sets — 7–2 and 7–0 to Bryant. Murray did not play badly, but was still unable to make any impression on his illustrious opponent. The finishing shot was a classic and left the audience gasping at the vision and artistry that was typical of Bryant. With the score 4–0 to Bryant in the second set, he held shot with a toucher close to the jack in the ditch. Murray had the second shot bowl a metre (yard) or so away from the jack. Bryant saw the possibilities of running his own second bowl — a toucher — into the ditch to count two and add a match-winning third by playing that final bowl powerfully enough to run on and settle just in front of Murray's best wood. It worked to perfection, getting the exact amount of weight needed to tie the match up and rub salt into the wounds the crown received that evening.

The Bryant performance was electrifying. The way in which he lined up a firing shot along his famous and unlit pipe, coupled with an aggressive stance that was like an animal going for the kill, brought gasps from the audience. He made the most of the occasion adding a touch of show business to his incredible skills and those odds against him winning the title came tumbling down again. Bryant brushed aside the challenge of Welshman Ray Hill in the next round in straight sets, although he was taken all the way before clinching the first. Bryant was into his third match before he dropped a set, and that was to nineteen-year-old Nigel Smith. There were echoes of another famous occasion as Smith took the second set 7–6, for he had beaten Bryant in a televised World Singles Championship semi-final eight months earlier. This time, Bryant gained his revenge, taking the third set 7–5 and then toppling Norma Shaw — the only lady bowler to progress beyond the second round — 7–3 and 7–3 to reach the final.

John Bell was among the fancied players in the top half of the draw in the 1984 *Superbowl* but the Cumbrian, a former rugby player until an injury forced him to stop, hit trouble in his opening game against the crown's Brian Duncan. Bell finally shook off the persistent Duncan to win that first set 7–5, only for the crown man to stick to his guns and win the second, 7–3. Duncan had been rated the top crown exponent but had little flat experience. He did, however, have a keen bowling brain and, having been a professional panel player in his early days, was not new to playing in front of enthusiastic and well-versed crowds. Backed by another huge Stage One audience, Preston's Duncan gave Bell a run for his money before losing the last set 7–3 to send a relieved Bell into a second round tie that did not present the same problems. Bell's next opponent was the Scotsman Davie Gourlay and he made few mistakes in a 7–4, 7–0 straight sets win that left the Scotsman a very disappointed player. But it sent Bell forward to meet another formidable crown challenger in Noel Burrows. Bell took the first and third sets by the same 7–3 scoreline. Burrows was sandwiched between these with a 7–4 success in the second set that was a taste of what was to come for the crown player the following year.

The semi-final pairing of Bell against the determined Scotsman Willie Wood had the makings of an almighty clash. Wood had been desperately unlucky in not winning the World Outdoor Singles when his opponent in the final, New Zealand's Peter Bellis, pipped him with a fluke shot at the last end. It was not surprising he felt that he was entitled to some luck, but it wasn't to come in *Superbowl*. Bell dealt comfortably with the Wood challenge with a straight sets success to clinch a final place against Bryant. The second year saw Wood gain his revenge with a straight sets win over Bell in the second round. Bell, by now describing his type of stance and delivery as 'sexy', had beaten Christine Knowles in the opening round. Bell took the first set, Bryant the next two — with only a point between them — in a match that started at 10.35 p.m. on Saturday 20 October and ended at 1.11 a.m. the next day, despite being only three sets. The closeness of the final extended the match to twenty-seven enthralling ends, kept spectators in their seats long after their normal bus services had ended, and pushed Granada into an over-run of one and a half hours in order to cover the entire final.

The men took twenty-six of the thirty-two places in the first *Superbowl* and were cut down to twenty-four in the second when the ladies' allocation was increased. The men set the woods rolling under house lights with a game that was not televised but which was to set the tone. Stan Frith, a crown player who had achieved the Grand Slam in winning three top titles in one season, met a Manchester-based Scot, Gordon Niven, who had had trials for England. Gordon was a member of the Heaton Hall and Bolton Clubs and he and his officials had been extremely helpful when preparations for putting the ambitious competition together first started. (Lancashire officials were also invited to take a leading part in handling that first *Superbowl*.) Gordon Niven was in the field on merit and he soon proved his pedigree. He had a long tussle with the Cheshire county captain, Frith — winner of the All-England, Champion of Champions and the Waterloo in 1983 — before winning 5–7, 7–6 and 7–2. Niven, a flat green bowler for thirty years, went on to beat Roy White in three sets before going out to Willie Wood in the quarter-final.

Roy White's career statistics make confusing reading as he is one of the rare breed who have played outdoors for Scotland and indoors for England. His nearest indoor club was Carlisle and that gave him an England qualification. Roy's first taste of *Superbowl* was an occasion that was equally confusing as he had to contend with the antics of the crown prince of laughter, the inimitable Vernon Lee, whose favourite trick is to chase his woods along the rink and dance in and out of the head as the bowl comes to rest. Quickstepping Vernon — the dancing master of crown green — got a few gentle reminders that this was not within the rules, and he became the first bowler in the competition warned to watch his step. 'I couldn't help myself. I just got carried away with the occasion', admitted Vernon after Ray had somehow kept his concentration on the game to win in two sets. The *Superbowl* experience inspired Vernon to join his local Blackpool indoor club, which was converted from an old circus training building. It opened less than a year after its creator, Mark Berry, caught the indoor bowling bug from attending Stage One. Vernon Lee was back for the second year, again losing in two sets, this time to Jim Baker in a cruel finish. An accurate firing shot, or that is what it appeared to be, brushed past its target to end the game.

The flat code provided a fair slice of entertaining characters, too, with Mal Hughes suggesting that his lively approach was going to unsettle Willie Wood. Hughes, the Hartlepool Dancer, came to Manchester as Manager of the Hartlepool Indoor Bowls Club and with a string of top successes to his credit. He appeared at the Commonwealth Games in Canada in 1978 and at the World Championships in Australia in 1980. A former double winner of the English indoor title, he took the first set off Wood but then lost the next two.

Former professional footballer, Bob Sutherland, was another who was tipped to go a long way. He had enjoyed a career playing soccer for Glasgow Rangers and, at the same time, achieved some success at bowls. He went on to win the British Isles indoor title in 1983 when he was also Scottish and World Champion. Bob's bowling career started in 1968 and two years later he won his club championship.

Michael Dunlop entered into the 'showbiz' spirit of *Superbowl.* He was a British Isles Indoor Champion at the tender age of twenty-four, having beaten David Bryant in the semi-final and then Russell Evans in the final. He was the youngest-ever bowler to appear in the Commonwealth Games when he played for Ireland at the age of eighteen. He lost to Noel Burrows in two sets in his opening game of the 1984 *Superbowl* but stayed on to become a firm friend of the crown players. Michael and Jim Baker were shrewd enough, however, to decline an invitation to take on a couple of crown players at their own game for a sidestake of several hundred pounds.

Richard Corsie brought more youthful flair to the Stage One scene when, at the age of only seventeen, he had the Scottish and British junior titles to his credit. Five years after starting to play, he won international honours with Scotland and his progress was so quick that he was described as the natural successor to Willie Wood. Corsie, from the Edinburgh Indoor Bowls Club, started well by slamming the crown's Michael Leach 7–1 and 7–2. Leach was the holder of the All-England title at the time, and skipper of the newly formed North Lancashire and Fylde county away team. However, he had played little flat and was caught by Corsie's precision play. Not even the lucky coin he keeps in his pocket when playing could help Leach. Corsie had another crown player in Robert Hitchen to remove — again in straight sets — before he found the skills of Norma Shaw in the quarter finals more than he could match.

Nigel Smith came up from the King George Indoor Bowls Club in Chessington, Surrey, with a reputation for turning on the style in front of the television cameras. He had produced a show-stopping performance when he beat David Bryant in the World Indoor Championships semi-finals in 1984, before losing to Jim Baker in the final. Nigel started with a two-set win over the crown's Norman Fletcher, who

On the way to a £1,000 cheque for the fastest finish is Jim Boyle starting his game against Nancy Gibson.

Tony Poole in a confident mood against Terry Sullivan.

Tony Poole during his game against Terry Sullivan.

A handshake signals Norman Fletcher's surprise win over Andy Ross.

showed some resistance in the second set but was generally outmanoeuvred. Smith then had the chance of repeating his win over Bryant, but the master was quick to make his mark with a first-set win. Smith, to his credit, refused to buckle and shook Bryant by taking the second set 7–6 and then taking five points before going down in the third.

The second *Superbowl* saw numerous changes in the flat green contingent as the players were selected mainly through winning qualifying competitions. Jim Boyle was anxious to improve his standing as an international player and he wasted no time in giving a warning of his form. He demolished Nancy Gibson 7–1 and 7–2 in the first game of the opening round. It was all over in seven ends and thirty-five minutes. Nobody could equal that for the fastest finish and Jim picked up the £1,000 special prize offered by sponsors Liverpool Victoria Insurance Company. Unfortunately, the game took place before television cover started and viewers missed the quickfire Boyle finish. Boyle, who plays for Whitburn Bowls Club (West Lothian) and West Lothian Indoor Bowls Club, had a tougher test in his next game and looked like going out when he dropped the opening set to Tony Allcock. He kept his head and finally got his reward by taking the next two sets to upset the odds. But the big man's time ran out in the quarter-finals where the consistency of Bryant proved too much. Bryant, borrowing Jimmy Davidson's heavier bowls, won in just nine ends. Boyle won his first event in 1960 when he took his club championship and he became an international outdoors player in 1972, a year after he received indoor honours. He was the Scottish Indoor Champion in 1976 and 1983.

David Cutler was the man who repeated the Bryant treatment when he faced Arthur Murray in a game that lasted only thirty-five minutes over ten ends. Cutler, quoted at 8–1 to win the event, whitewashed the unfortunate Murray in the first set and went on to win the second set 7–2, moving forward as clear favourite against Jeanette Conlan at the next stage. Cutler, a player since 1968, was reckoned by many to be the most consistent outdoor singles player in England. He had a very precise style characterized by standing upright on the mat and delivering off a strong step forward. He took the first set off Jeanette but was pipped in the next two in one of the tournament's biggest upsets.

Odds of 5–1 on were being offered when Terry Sullivan stepped on to the rink to play the crown's Tony Poole. Sullivan was the World and United Kingdom Champion and a 12–1 shot to win the title while Poole was an outsider at 40–1. It looked as though these odds were justified when the confident Sullivan raced into a 6–1 lead, but Poole came all the way back to take the first set. It was 6–1 to Poole in the second set before Sullivan scored again and fell to a stunning 7–6, 7–2 defeat.

Willie Wood invested in a stronger set of bowls when he played in *Superbowl* for the second time. It proved to be a shrewd switch as scarcely anybody could compete with Wood's line and length. He did not drop a set until losing to Burrows in the semi-final. Wood, a player since 1951, has twice reached the semi-finals and finished fourth after a play-off with Norma Shaw in the first year. He demonstrated his concern about the effectiveness of his bowls by dashing back to his hotel to change a set before he played Norma — then he lost. But the second time around, Willie judged it better and looked like going all the way to the final. The match against Burrows hinged on a vital measure that gave the crown man a treble to take the game.

Andy Ross's first encounter with a crown green bowler was not a happy experience for this English Indoor Singles Champion of 1984. He came up against the striking power of Norman Fletcher and was 6–1 down before he knew it. Ross settled down to come back with a treble, only to find Fletcher winning the first set at the next end without needing to send his last bowl. Ross, who qualified for *Superbowl* by winning the British Isles Singles Championship, came back to win the second set 7–2 after Fletcher had struck superbly to stop a possible full hand with the scores 1–1. The last set saw Fletcher get to the longer marks that best suited his crown green style and he won 7–2. Ross, a book sales representative, plays for the Longmeadow Indoor Bowls Club and is the only Anglo-Scot to win the English Indoor Singles.

The blond, curly hair and good looks of Tony Allcock won over the ladies in Stage One when the likeable England international appeared in the 1985 *Superbowl*. More important, his skills on the rink made him a favourite with the whole audience. Allcock came with the weight of the 'new David Bryant' tag on his shoulders and he looked the part as he dismissed the crown's Robert Hitchen in straight sets on the opening morning. Scotsman Jim Boyle ended Allcock's challenge in the next game and there was general disappointment among the bowling fraternity that the thirty-year-old had not progressed further. But Allcock's day was soon to come as he went on to win the World Indoor Singles title and then, with David Bryant, added the World Pairs title. Tony, England's youngest-ever skip, qualified for the *Superbowl* as the National Singles Champion. He is a member of the Cotswold Indoor Bowls Club.

Jim Baker's sensible handling of the Vernon Lee situation, as the little man turned on his dancing act, helped to make him a firm favourite with the fans. He kept his control to remove Lee in straight sets and repeated the treatment against Richard Brittan, a young crown bowler with flat experience. Many thought that Baker, who opened as a 6–1 shot, was on course for the final stages when he played Jeanette Conlan in the second game on the rink on 18 October 1985. The prize for the winner was a place in the semi-finals, but second-favourite Baker went out as the gritty Conlan produced another show-stopping performance in straight sets. Baker is the manager of the Jim Baker Bowls Centre in Templepatrick, County Antrim, and is a most accomplished indoor bowler. He was Irish Champion in 1981, 1983 and 1985, British Isles Champion in 1981, World Indoor Runner-up in 1982, and World Champion in 1984. He skipped the Irish team to the World triples at twenty-two years old, and is the youngest international skip in bowling history. Jim has a dangerous habit of starting slowly and that can be costly in the sets game; that, however, did not seem to bother him when he went on to win the United Kingdom Singles.

Frank McCartney is another personality from bowling's 'bright young brigade'; he won a place in *Superbowl* on the strength of his National Indoor Singles win. Frank, who comes from Ayrshire, plays for the Dreghorn Club outdoors and the Irvine Indoor Bowls Club. He faced a tough opening game with a crown opponent, Brian Duncan. Frank is an indoor specialist and showed no fear of taking Duncan on the longer marks that the crown players favoured. He took the first set 7–4 but lost the second, 7–3. Then, he showed great composure by staving off a strong Duncan rally in the final set, and he deserved his 7–5 success. That win under his belt, the young Scot went on to meet and beat Norma Shaw by winning the first and third sets by convincing 7–1 margins, sandwiching a 7–2 second set in between. McCartney put in plenty of practice on the rink for his quarter-final against Noel Burrows and this time his good fortune came to an end. Burrows romped through to win the first set and then still proved he had the edge, although McCartney forced him to 7–6 in the second.

Rodney McCutcheon was another outstanding youngster. At twenty-three, he already enjoyed considerable success: the Irish Outdoor Under 25 in 1981, the British Isles Junior Outdoor in 1982, and the Irish Junior title twice. He plays for Belfast Indoor Bowls Club and had the misfortune to take on Noel Burrows in the first round. At one set each, McCutcheon was eager to upset Burrows' style in the crucial set but he was never allowed a finger-grip on the deciding set, and Burrows stormed through to take the set 7–1.

Over the first two years, the crown contingent featured a number who were specialists at their own version of bowls and who were given a couple of bites at the *Superbowl*. Stan Frith was an obvious choice after completing the grand slam in the crown world — the All-England, Waterloo and Champion of Champions titles in 1983. His economic style, with a preference for medium marks gave him the ammunition to make a good show. Against him was the fact that he had had little opportunity to play flat and certainly not at the level demanded by *Superbowl*. Nonetheless, he gave Gordon Niven a run, winning the first set of *Superbowl* 7–5, but then losing the next two. Frith was back to meet Norma Shaw in the second year and was disappointed to go out in straight sets, recognizing that the experienced Stockton player had given him a lesson in tactics. Stan came in as

Noel Burrows and Rodney McCutcheon waiting for the result of a measure.

Above and right Jeanette Conlan sees Len Higginbottom's final wood fall short.

The unusual action of Michael Robinson.

an Owley Wood Club player and as skipper of Cheshire's county side. By the second year, he was also a registered player with the Swinton Indoor Club.

Vernon Lee is now a regular player at the new Blackpool Indoor Club, which has five rinks in a converted building that was once used to train animal acts for Blackpool Tower Circus. His appearances in any television competition are full of life, good humour and skill. His tactics, which include chasing after the bowls and sometimes throwing his duster at his opponent's woods in joking disgust, are all part of his act. Yet that does not disguise Lee's talent. He has won the Waterloo, the North Lancashire and Fylde Merit, the Yorkshire Bank Crown King, the Tetley Open and was once a regular player on the professional panel.

Brian Duncan has earned the rating as the crown game's number one player over the years. That title is due to his remarkable consistency, and his ability to read even the most difficult of crown greens quickly and spot opportunities to make his wood count. That sort of talent also makes him a flat green player to be respected, and he reached the semi-finals of the United Kingdom Indoor Championships at his home town, Preston, in 1984. He lost both his opening games in the first two *Superbowls* but succeeded in taking sets off John Bell and Frank McCartney. Duncan plays for the Railway Hotel Club in Lostock Hall, near Preston, and is a member of the indoor club at Blackpool. His many tournament wins include the Waterloo, the Bass Masters, the Top Crown and the Lancashire Merit.

Norman Fletcher often pairs up with Duncan and they make up a formidable team, probably the best in the crown game. Fletcher, like Duncan, learned his trade on the old professional panel and that makes him an aggressive, gritty performer. He is one of the best players at reading an end and deciding which wood is counting, even if it is only by a fraction. If Fletcher says a wood is in, opponents rarely bother to call on the measurers. He has been playing since 1955 but it was eleven years before his first win of note. Since then, he has scarcely completed a season without a major win. His successes include the Greenall County Classic, the Chesters G.E.C. Classic and the Lancashire Merit. He fell in the first round of the first *Superbowl* to Nigel Smith, whose masking of the jack often prevented Fletcher using his fearsome firing shots. 'I was a mug', he said, and lived up to his promise to improve when he beat Andy Ross and then rattled the mighty David Bryant in an electrifying second-round game. He plays for the Bowling Green (Leigh) but does not belong to an indoor club.

Spear-heading the crown attack was the versatile Noel Burrows. As well as being a top crown player, he had also enjoyed success at ten-pin bowling and won a major target bowls competition before stepping across to the flat scene. His determination to succeed at whichever sport he takes up contributed towards Burrows reaching the *Superbowl* quarter-finals in the first year. He was the crown player to go the furthest in the competition that year. His win in the second year gave the crown game — and the flat — the biggest boost for years. It gave the crown players the encouragement to try their hands seriously at the other code and it gave flat bowling a considerable foothold in the traditional crown areas. Burrows became involved in the launching of the world's biggest indoor bowls centre — fourteen rinks at Bowlers in Manchester's industrial complex Trafford Park. He moved out of the Red Lion Hotel in Withington, where his family had been landlords for three generations, made the big step into the flat world, and backed his judgement by becoming General Manager of Bowlers. Burrows has won the Waterloo, the All-England, Champion of Champions, the Bass Masters, and most of the big handicaps. He now plays crown for Sale Excelsior and flat for his own Bowlers Club. This player has made so much progress at flat that he has had trials for England.

Mick Robinson is the Yorkshire left-hander with a very low delivery style and a crab-like release of the bowl that makes him a difficult opponent. He won the English Open at Blackburn and made many Yorkshire appearances. His journey into the flat world has won him a place in the Huddersfield indoor team and outdoors he plays for Morton House (Dewsbury). In *Superbowl* he went out in straight sets twice in the first round, first to Bob Sutherland and then to David Bryant. Interestingly, a comparison of both players' style revealed similarities at the point of delivery.

Arthur Murray is one of only two players to have won the famous Waterloo title twice. Arthur, who retired early and was able to concentrate on bowling, took the Waterloo in 1973 and 1978 equalling the record of Bernard Kelly of Hyde. He has won most things in the crown game and switched to indoor play at Swinton and then at the Manchester Bowlers Club. However, his experience in *Superbowl* has been painful, as he was removed at the first round by David Bryant and David Cutler. If dedication and determination to succeed count for anything, then Arthur Murray will make his mark in the flat game. He plays crown for L. and M. (Altrincham).

Len Higginbottom has had little luck at *Superbowl,* losing three sets to Jim Baker and then losing again in three sets to Jeanette Conlan. All this, when the turn over of a bowl in both matches could have given him victory. He has caught the flat bug and regularly spends up to six hours in practice sessions at the Blackpool Indoor Club. Higginbottom, a lecturer in electrical engineering, has won the Bass Masters, the Waterloo Spring title and many tough handicaps around the North West. He is Lancashire county skipper and plays for Green Inn (Leigh) and Swinton and Blackpool indoor clubs.

There is a strip of turf on the famous Waterloo green at Blackpool that is known as Poole's patch. It is a strip about 25.6 metres (28 yards) long that runs diagonally across the green and marks the ground on which Tony Poole won such titles as the Champion of Champions and B.B.C. Masters. Poole's preference for this sort of length makes him a suitable candidate for the flat game and he demonstrated this by beating Terry Sullivan in straight sets in *Superbowl* 1985. A Shropshire county regular, Poole also plays for Castlefields (Shrewsbury).

Robert Hitchen has won many top crown titles but failed to make much headway when he appeared in the first two *Superbowls*. He beat the crown's Steve Nixon on his first appearance and then fell to Richard Corsie. The following year, he went straight out to Tony Allcock. Hitchen, left-handed, has enjoyed considerable success on the crown with wins in the Chesters G.E.C. Classic, the Champion of Champions, the Top Pairs and the Yorkshire County Merit in successive years. He is the first player to achieve this. A determined character, he was banned by his home town association for playing in the televised pairs event instead of a local event. Hitchen plays for Akroyd Park (Halifax) and the indoor club at Huddersfield.

Richard Brittan was something of an unknown to the *Superbowl* audience even though he was a crown player. He burst on the scene with six straight wins for his Warwickshire and Worcestershire county team. That was after winning the Sutton Coldfield Individual Merit at the age of sixteen. In 1984, he won the Midlands Masters and lost in this competition's final, the following year, to Tony Poole. He plays for Sutton Park (Sutton Coldfield) and Erdington Court Indoor Club.

Allan Thompson first played indoor bowls at the age of twelve — but that was an indoor crown green that was laid on a special frame at Huddersfield. He is a founder member of the Huddersfield Indoor Club and was expected to go a long way in *Superbowl*. But Thompson lost in his first game to Richard Brittan in a three-setter. Thompson's crown success includes the *Manchester Evening News* Men's Open, and he has made sixty county appearances for Yorkshire. Thompson plays for Mirfield Old Bank and the Huddersfield Indoor Club.

Harold Barlow is the pride of Manchester. A superb striker, fine team-man and prolific winner of sixteen invitation events around Manchester, he found the switch to flat too much of an ordeal. The former professional footballer went out in straight sets to Davie Gourlay in the first *Superbowl* before a sympathetic audience who were there to encourage one of the crown's finest ambassadors. Harold plays for Openshaw A.E.U. in Manchester.

The windmill style of Michael Leach and his fondness for short marks should have made this Preston solicitor a formidable flat opponent. There was little chance to assess his true ability on the rink as he went straight out to Richard Corsie. Leach started playing bowls at the age of five and went on to become All-England Champion in 1984. He was North Lancashire and Fylde captain but hit problems with his game in 1986 and stepped down to rediscover his best form. Leach plays for Hope Street Recreation Club in St Annes-on-Sea and is a member of the Blackpool Indoor Club.

The youthful promise of crown's Steve Nixon earned him a place in the 1984 line-up at the age of twenty-two. One of Cheshire's brightest prospects, Steve had won his county's junior title and had reached the finals of several top handicaps. He managed to take a set off Robert Hitchen before losing. Nixon plays for Owley Wood Recreation Club in Weaverham.

PLAYERS – LADIES

Crown green player, Diane Priestley, from Bradford.

Jeanette Conlan in action.

The inclusion of ladies in the *Superbowl* field was a feature demanded by Granada right from the initial planning stages. It was a decision that was greeted by the male section with raised eyebrows and shaking of heads. But there is no doubt that the ladies have proved their value both in terms of ability and entertainment. They have brought to *Superbowl* a touch of glamour and an element of anticipation that have knitted in richly to the overall fabric of the competition. In the first year, the ladies were allocated six places — three to the flat and three to the crown code. By the second year, their share had increased to eight places in the field of thirty-two players.

Jeanette Conlan came to Manchester as the Scottish Singles Champion and holder of the British Isles title but the Scottish woman was still an unkown, so far as the majority of the *Superbowl* Stage One audiences were concerned. By the second afternoon of the 1985 event, Jeanette was already well on the way to becoming the biggest character to emerge from the competition cast list, which read like a bowling *Who's Who*. Her first game was tough; it was against a crown green favourite, the college lecturer Len Higginbottom. The first signs that there was a major crown setback on the cards came when Higginbottom, winner of a host of top events, lost the first set 7–4. Jeanette, a thirty-eight-year-old food process chargehand and mother of a fifteen-year-old son, was displaying the determination, enthusiasm and bubbling personality that was to become her trademark. She took Higginbottom on with a fierce attack of precision play and lethal driving that impressed her opponent and audience alike. Higginbottom drew on the years of experience gained on the tough handicap circuit of crown green to keep a grip on the game and he roared back with a 7–2 second set win to square the match. If ever Jeanette's temperament was to be tested, it was in that first round game. She rose to the occasion in a classic final set to gain a 7–6 success that established her as a crowd favourite. With that sort of backing inside Stage One, Jeanette was well-armed to go forward and make a mockery of the odds of 33–1 that were offered against her when the competition started.

Jeanette had a lot going for her as a study by sports scientists supported. An analysis by the British Society of Sports Sciences and by top specialist Jenny Halfon indicated that Jeanette had the attributes to become the best bowler in Britain. Women normally have a lower centre of gravity than men and this coupled with her extra arm-length — they are 5cm (2 in) longer than average — helped Jeanette develop an impeccable style of delivery. Her driving shot was an effective ploy and was to be demonstrated with great success against David Cutler and Jim Baker. 'Jeanette has plenty of nervous energy that she enjoys using', said Mrs Halfon in an interview in the *Daily Telegraph*. 'She knows how to turn up trumps when the going gets tough and uses her guts for guidance.'

The going certainly got tough when Jeanette faced the England international player, David Cutler, at lunchtime on Thursday, 17 October. The Stage One audience that day had come in the hope of seeing an upset but never seriously believed it would happen. Cutler, a serious character as befits an Inland Revenue Official, took the first set 7–5 but had reason for concern as Jeanette's determination made it clear that this was no foregone conclusion. She rattled the man, who had won every outdoor single title available, to such an extent that at one end he gestured one of her bowls through the head — a habit frowned on in the flat world, although it is a harmless feature in crown. Jeanette took the next two sets 7–5 and 7–6, in a tingling game, to move into the quarter-finals and a massive test against the 1984 World Champion, Jim Baker. Another breath-taking, two-set triumph — by 7–3 and 7–5 — sent Jeanette breezing along into the semi-finals and a showdown with the game's greatest name, David Bryant. This was the end for Jeanette as Bryant showed no mercy with a 7–0 and 7–2 win. It was his second semi-finals win against a lady bowler — he beat Norma Shaw in the first year.

Jeanette Conlan plays for the Midlothian Indoor Bowls Club, having switched to indoor bowls in November 1980, five years after starting her outdoor career. She became an indoor specialist and her progress was so remarkable that she won the Scottish Singles title in 1985, following with the British Isles title. She became a Scottish international player in 1984. Her son, Paul, had won the Midlothian Junior Championship twice by the time he was fifteen years old.

Norma Shaw took to the rarified Stage One atmosphere so well that she reached the semi-finals in the first year, where she beat Willie Wood to land the third place. She struck the first major blow for the ladies by toppling Jim Baker, who was then the World Indoor Champion. Rated the world's number one lady player for years, Norma has represented England at outdoor and indoor bowls. Her omission from the outdoor team in 1986 came as a shock both to Norma and to her many admirers. Her first achievement was winning the Tees-side Outdoor Champion of Champions event and she has gone on to success in most of the leading competitions indoors and outdoors, including world and commonwealth games events whether they be singles, pairs or triples. Her clubs are Tees-side Indoor Bowls Club and outdoors, Norton and Ropner Park.

Julie Davies won over the Stage One audience with a display of precision play, a positive approach and an infectious sense of humour. This combination went down so well that nobody could complain about the way she dealt with the enormous promise of the crown's Karen Galvin. Julie brought the Welsh Outdoor Singles title — won a month earlier — to Manchester in October 1985, and was in top form as she opened with a 7–1 first set return against Karen, a young crown player who had impressed people in the first *Superbowl*. The second set was tougher but eventually Julie won through 7–5. She had the benefit of some advice on the *Superbowl* rinks behaviour from her Port Talbot clubmate, Ray Hill, who had appeared in the inaugural competition. A difficult game — against another crown player, Noel Burrows — faced Julie in the second round but she again looked confident as she won the first set, 7–6. Burrows came back with 7–3 and 7–6 (on a measure) scorelines to go through a relieved player, while a disappointed Julie was left to regret not going for winners on a couple of occasions instead of playing for safety. She is a member of the Port Talbot Ladies Bowls Club and started playing in 1976. Two years later, Julie won the Swansea Ladies Open Outdoor Singles and the following year had success in the British Isles Fours. She was Welsh National Singles Champion in 1983 and losing finalist in the British Isles Outdoor Singles a year later. She is a Welsh international player, indoors and out, and represented her country in singles and pairs in the World Championships in Melbourne in 1985.

Nancy Gibson's experience of the *Superbowl* rink lasted only thirty-five minutes and ran to only seven ends. This Northern Ireland veteran player — the oldest competitor at the age of sixty-four — was on the receiving end of a 7–1, 7–2 defeat by Scotland's Jim Boyle. Nancy Gibson, who plays bowls for relaxation, is a founder member of the Lisnagarvey Club in County Antrim. Highlights of a career that started in 1957 outdoors and ten years later indoors are skipping the winning rink in the British Isles Fours in 1974, winning the National Singles title and skipping her club to the National Indoor Pairs title three times in five years.

Sarah Gourlay was the British Isles Indoor Singles Champion in 1984 and that was more than good enough to earn the Ayrshire housewife a place in the first *Superbowl* field. She beat the crown's Freda Locke in straight sets in her opening game but then fell by the same scores — 7–1 and 7–5 — in her next game to the nineteen-year-old Nigel Smith. Sarah and husband Davie were the first husband-and-wife pairing to be invited into *Superbowl*, and were both given world rankings at the same time in 1984. She won the Scottish Pairs in 1968 and has represented her country. She comes from Mossblown and plays for Prestwick Indoor Bowls Club.

Sarah Gourlay heads for a two-set win over Freda Locke.

Freda Locke in action.

Karen Galvin, the pride of the crown green ladies world.

Tony Poole keeps a close watch on a delivery by Sylvia Jones.

Jean Valls was taken by surprise when she took on the twenty-year-old Karen Galvin, a young player with considerable crown success but with no real experience of the flat game. The audience was strongly behind the younger player and Jean, then the British Isles and English Outdoor Singles Champion, found the occasion, on the Tuesday afternoon of the first competition, something of an ordeal. She lost 7–5 and 7–4 to the surprise of the flat contingent and to the delight of Karen's army of supporters. An England international player, outdoors and indoors, Jean is from Morden, Surrey, and her club is Richmond Indoor Bowls Club.

Two crown green ladies were selected for both the 1984 and 1985 *Superbowls*, Karen Galvin and Christine Knowles. Karen, from Warrington, has been playing crown since she was fourteen years old and only four years later she won the toughest of the ladies competitions — their own version of the famous Waterloo at Blackpool. She became interested in the game when she accompanied her parents to watch them play and took up the game herself. She was the youngest winner of the Ladies Waterloo and she confirmed her potential by also taking the Wyre Festival title at Fleetwood in the same year. Karen plays for the Thames Board Club in Warrington and plays indoor flat at Swinton on the outskirts of Manchester. She has become a keen flat competitor and also plays outdoors for the Bolton Club, sometimes partnering the Scottish-born England trialist Gordon Niven, who played in the first *Superbowl*. A left-hander, Karen qualified for the National Singles in 1985 as a Lancashire representative — further evidence of her successful conversion to the flat code. Karen lost 7–5 and 7–0 to Noel Burrows in

Christine Knowles enjoys competing against men and she was the first lady to get an entry into the normally all-male Waterloo Handicap.

the second round of the first *Superbowl*. In the second year, she proved to be no match for Julie Davies and fell 7–1 and 7–5.

Christine Knowles brought a controversial touch to *Superbowl*. After all, she was the lady who managed to get an entry into the normally all-male Waterloo Handicap at Blackpool, only to be ordered to go off the green and change from 'hot pants' into a pair of trousers so as not to distract her male opponents! She has strong views about ladies bowls, describing them as 'a load of tea and fairy cakes'. She is an aggressive player who shows no fear of taking on the men at their own game. Christine did not win a game in the first two *Superbowls*, although the 7–3 and 7–0 defeat by a sporting Ray Hill was a cruel scoreline. The admirable Ray even took Christine down to the local club at Swinton to coach her before they played their *Superbowl* game. By the time the second *Superbowl* came round, Christine had teamed up with Karen Galvin to win the Swinton Indoor Ladies Pairs and was better equipped to deal with the mighty John Bell. She astounded the critics by taking the first set 7–2 before the slow-to-start Bell hit back and won the next two, 7–3 and 7–1.

The third member of the crown ladies trio in the first year was Freda Locke, nominated as a player with considerable success. She was rated the crown player with the style best suited to the flat game, but that counted for little as Freda went out in her first game in straight sets to Sarah Gourlay. Freda plays for Muirhead Bowls Club in Liverpool and she won the Isle of Man festival in 1978 and 1983 as well as the All-England title in 1982.

The draw for the opening round in the second year gave crown ladies Sylvia Jones and Diane Priestley a game against each other. Sylvia, from Malpas in Cheshire, won a marathon match that lasted for three close sets. It was played under house lights and was not transmitted on television. Sylvia plays in three crown green leagues and for North Shropshire. She reached seven finals in the summer before her *Superbowl* appearance. Diane's first crown green achievement was winning the Golden Lady Yorkshire Bank title in 1984. She comes from Bradford and plays for Cleckheaton S.C., Oakenshaw Park (Bradford) and Crow Nest Park (Dewsbury).

TONY ALLCOCK

Tony Allcock signing autographs.

The tills at the Ladbrokes betting counter, in the imposing foyer of Stage One, were kept busy from the moment the bookmakers quoted Tony Allcock at 8–1 to win the second *Superbowl* title. The punters like the Allcock style — busy and confident — and they ignored the fact that he was in the same half of the draw as the hot 5–2 favourite David Bryant. Allcock, headmaster of an education centre for mentally handicapped adults, was obliged to decline an invitation to play in the opening *Superbowl*, but he was there in 1985 when he was among the early starters in the competition. There was a lot of money riding on Allcock when he stepped on to the rink for a first-round game against the crown's Robert Hitchen, a neat, left-handed player from Halifax in Yorkshire. Allcock was quickly into his stride, leading well and having too much all-round experience for the unlucky Hitchen. A straight sets win — 7–2 and 7–1 — sent Allcock forward to the second round and immediately knocked a couple of points off his odds.

Allcock was the crown green audience's sort of player. He exuded confidence and had a presence on the rink that appeared to be worth a couple of chalks start over any opponent prepared to be overawed. Yet Allcock himself gives a very different view of his inner feelings whenever he plays a game. His words reveal a fascinating excursion into the mind of one of bowling's more profound characters:

> I used to play a lot of competition cards and I believe that gave me a discipline that has been of great benefit in bowls. In cards at that level you must remember which ones have been played before, and in bowls it can be equally as important during a game to recall which shots you have tried, and with what sort of result, against an opponent. I firmly believe that it is, however, more important to be aware of your own strengths than necessarily of your opponent's weaknesses. Play to those strengths and do not allow your play to be dominated by worrying too much about your opponent. Moving the mat around is something I have made great use of at times, in certain situations. If I have played a three-quarter jack and been a yard through, I might try to adjust by moving the mat back at the next opportunity. Sometimes that can be counter-productive as it could suit your opponent, too.

Allcock, the player tipped to take over David Bryant's number one mantle, has all the outward appearances of a man very much in control of things. He has the natural air of a champion, the gift of winning an audience's support, and it seemed he had so much going for him that *Superbowl* should have been his stage. He was odds-on to beat the amiable Scotsman Jim Boyle in the second round and he opened with a bustling, breezy first set win by 7–2. That was the end of Allcock's success for his game started to crumble and Boyle stepped in to take the second set 7–2. He then held off Allcock's efforts to get back into the game and was a worthy 7–4 third-set winner to take the second-round game.

Allcock was left to carry out his usual inquest on his personal performance, and he was extremely critical of his own preparation:

I'm not one for making excuses but I do analyse most things I do. If I have a bad day in my work, I will go over the problems, every little hiccup. I try to relax and get things clear in my mind. Everybody should get to know themselves. I have learned what is good for me and what isn't and I did a silly thing before I played Jim. Stage One is close to the famous *Coronation Street* set in Granada's complex and I wanted to bring my parents up from Leicester to see it. I thought it was a fairly easy car-drive from Manchester to Leicester and back and I tried to do it on the day I played. The distance was far more than I realized and then we hit a traffic jam on the way to Manchester. I was rushed and not able to organize myself as I would have liked. It taught me a lesson in preparation and while I may not have won the game had I been better organized, I now set out to try to eliminate areas which could give me problems. Learning from that experience, I am sure, helped me to go on and win the Embassy World Indoor title after *Superbowl*. I did not hang around after I had played games in World Championships. I spent my spare time quietly and I timed my arrival a lot better.

That sort of thinking was a crucial factor in Allcock going on to win the World Indoor Singles title at Coatbridge and then teaming up with David Bryant to add the World Pairs title at Bournemouth. These successes follow his triumphs in the 1980 World Triples and the 1984 World Fours. Yet he admits to the sort of pre-match feelings that can affect the average club player:

As a boy I was trained as a solo singer and won numerous trophies; despite the fact that I had nerves before I went on stage, they soon disappeared. It is the same whenever I play bowls, with the pre-match nerves still there until I actually start playing. I believe I have a slight inferiority complex before every game I play. I am always anxious not to make a fool of myself. I am determined to keep the game tight and I never underestimate an opponent. There have been times when nerves have also started to nag at me during the game. A typical example was when I played Noel Burrows in the World Singles and I had built an unbelievable lead of 18–1. He started to come back at me and I was beginning to let myself worry. Could he actually come back all the way? I remember thinking. But then I told myself to think clearly and forget him and just carry on playing as I had earlier in the game. Finally it all came right for me. Playing against Noel and the crown green bowlers can be difficult for the flat players. This is what I have described as being their unpredictable play in situations that, historically in flat, call for certain shots. We have what we call the percentage shot but the crown players traditionally come from another direction and their percentage shot is not necessarily the flat one. Noel Burrows, in particular, has done well in changing to flat but I feel that crown green players will go through a difficult period after switching. They will have to come to terms with the overall demands of the flat game and its tactics. But once they have done that they will be a force, as they are fine, natural bowlers with few inhibitions.

The Allcock style of delivery is one he has developed over the years, often to the concern of coaches. He explains:

It's one that suits me but I do accept that I do not follow the general rule at the point of delivery. I believe that I have everything right according to the text book up to that point but then I check the release of the bowl and I do not follow through in the accepted style. It's as though I were putting at golf. I get to the point of contact and there is a check, instead of following through in the generally accepted way. I think the style may have come from my early days when, at the age of about eight, I used to play on my father's lawn. I often used eight bowls and sometimes bowled left-handed to set up heads. But it was fast-running and I had to hold back to keep the bowls on the lawn. That could have been the point at which my checking style developed.

The style may not be copybook but it has served Allcock well, taking him to the World title at the age of only thirty. He has experimented over the years with various weights and makes of bowls, and is delighted with the set made for him by Australia's famous bowls-maker, Bruce Hensel, of which he says:

It is like anything else in life, you get what you pay for when you look for a new set of bowls. New players face quite a dilemma but I would suggest they did as I did by experimenting until they are happy. In my case, I sent out a request to Australia to try to get a set made similar to some David Bryant had used. When I went out to play in the Australian Masters in 1985, Bruce Hensel had made me the set and I liked them as soon as I tried them. I played with them in the Masters but then decided to ship them back home, instead of carrying them with my luggage. They got lost and it was August before I received them, so up 'til then I had, for me, a fairly lean time. I use the bowls indoors and out and they have been successful.

Allcock's second-round exit from the 1985 *Superbowl* at least allowed him the consolation of stepping into the shoes of television commentator and observer. He came into the commentary box to join Hugh Johns, Jimmy Davidson, David Bryant and myself and helped us round off the six days by working on the hour-long highlights programme enjoyed in the Granada region. Tony Allcock's ability to adjust to the demands of the television studio was so impressive that he was invited back for the 1986 show. Granada Head of Sport Paul Doherty believes that Allcock has the ideal image to be projected as a commentator. 'He picks up things quickly and is as good as any sporting personality who has tried to become a commentator.' Allcock gets an invitation as a player on the strength of his World title. He sums up:

The *Superbowl* is the most professional bowling tournament I have ever been to. The players' interests are of paramount interest to Granada and that can only be good for the game. The sets also suit my style of play. You must tune in immediately as it is a 100-yard sprint with enormous concentration.

NOEL BURROWS

Noel Burrows with the trophy after winning Superbowl *1985.*

Noel Burrows took the first tentative steps along the road that was to lead to *Superbowl* stardom, in May 1980, in the crown green setting of the Lloyds Hotel, Chorlton-cum-Hardy, in the Manchester suburbs. The occasion was the opening heat of the *Manchester Evening News* men's competition and Burrows was hard pushed to even get through the first round. He was struggling at 19–17 down but raised his game to win; he went on to win two more games and reached the sub-final stages of a competition that attracted more than 1,000 entries. Two months later, Burrows flew back from a holiday in New York having qualified for the final sixteen of the *News* event. He was suffering from jet lag and had to play, without practice, on the Stretford G.E.C. green when he had not had a game of bowls for more than a fortnight. It was a mark of his natural ability that Burrows was able to conquer tiredness to beat some of the best crown green bowlers in the game. He won the *Evening News* title and all that went with the success in a prestigious event. Burrows then went on to represent the *Evening News* in the Champion of Champions competition at the Waterloo, Blackpool, still unaware that the door to a whole new world was about to open to him.

He won the Champions title and on the strength of that was invited into his first flat green competition. It was the John Player Invitation at Darlington with prize money donated by the tobacco company (which had also sponsored the Champions event at Blackpool). 'That was my first experience of flat green bowling and it got right to my taste buds', recalled Burrows. 'I remember beating Norma Shaw in my group and losing to the English and Irish champions to finish fifth overall. I had never experienced anything like that sort of bowling. For a player who had spent his life in crown green to face people, who had been only names to me, at their own game was a rare opportunity.' Burrows returned to Manchester with his eyes opened to new opportunities of developing his considerable bowling skills. Life as landlord of the Red Lion Hotel, Withington, where there is a crown green, was never the same as Burrows determined that he would give this flat game serious consideration.

He found a willing helper in Gordon Niven, a Scot who had been through England trials at the flat game, and played on Manchester's only rinks — at Heaton Park. Burrows joined Niven as a member of the Huddersfield Indoor Club, which was across the Pennines in Yorkshire. He competed in the English National Singles and was then invited to play in the United Kingdom Championships in Preston in 1983, where he reached the second round. Burrows has played in the United Kingdom competition three times and was never able to get further than the second round. The crown green contingent got into that competition by playing a qualifying session at Carlisle, sixteen of them chasing four places. Tony Poole, Allan Thompson and Mick Robinson were the other crown green men to join Burrows in that first United Kingdom Championships appearance. 'At no time, in those days, was I able to get in enough practice at the flat game and this has been a problem we have all faced until the formation of more flat green centres in the North West', said Burrows.

He uses his own personal experience to draw on, giving advice to any crown green player wanting to take the same steps into the flat world:

They will probably find that they have to adjust their stance and delivery, as the accentuated back-swing most crown green players have is not necessary in flat, where the carpet is much quicker than the grass they normally play on. I adopt a stooped stance on the mat and I have slowed down my delivery style. The delivery should be a gentle push from the elbow as opposed to a swing from the elbow. Players should also be aware of the advantages that can be gained from using the mat. A delivery from the front of the mat compared with from the back is a difference of a couple of feet in the flat game. This can be important and I have found that on certain marks I can get the angle I want from taking up a position at the back of the footer. In crown green bowls, the footer is so small that there is little advantage to be gained.

When it comes to choosing sets of bowls with which to play the flat game, here is the Burrows recommendation. Do not buy a set until you have tried a few out. Make sure you are happy with them and find them particularly suitable for firing. He explains, 'I have two sets of bowls for the flat game as I have for crown. They are the same weight, but one set have a narrow draw and the other wider drawing bowls.' Burrows, the perfectionist, places great importance on practice and reveals that even in the flat game he uses a routine he learned from one of the crown game's finest ever bowlers, Bill Dawber, who won the Waterloo Handicap in 1959. Burrows explains:

Bill taught me how to play against myself. I would use my two sets of crown green bowls as though I were playing an opponent and trying to out-think him. I do the same thing with my two flat green sets, sending down six bowls first to build up a head, but then firing with my last two. One problem crown green players will face is the switch from the bowls they have been used to, weighing around 2 lb 13 oz (1.3 kg) and then using the flat bowls at 3 lb 5 oz (1.5 kg). I have learned that you cannot play both games in one day, which I did in the first year of *Superbowl*. When the second one came around, I had already decided to put my crown green bowls away and I stopped playing a fortnight before *Superbowl* simply to concentrate on practising.

Burrows was to be found practising on the *Superbowl* rink in Stage One at the quietest times, working on his game before joining his colleagues in general practice sessions. He believes:

All bowling is down to basic skill but the most important lesson I have learned over the past years is that you have to be prepared to be humble and listen. The problem with many crown green bowlers is that we all want to be skip and we all think we know best when, in fact, we really do not know enough about the flat green game and we must be prepared to learn first. I have been fortunate in that the competitions I have played in have been against top flat green players. I have been given lessons during these games, just by watching them in action. Tony Allcock is a player I admire and he has said that he thinks I am an unpredictable player. This is because I use my general knowledge of bowls and play the game as I think best. If my opponent in a flat game is trying to guard against something, for instance, I will try to outwit him by delivering a bowl that is quite different from what he is anticipating.

Fitness in playing the longer flat game is something that Burrows has had to pay particular attention to during his short time in the other code. He says:

Crown green bowlers can feel exhausted during a flat game, and not only because they take much longer than matches they are used to. There is also the effect artificial lighting can have. One tip I picked up was to take time out during the playing of a head and sit down at the side with my gaze away from the rink. I found this eased the strain for a few moments. We are also playing the flat game too quickly because of our years in crown green where it is sometimes an advantage to get your bowls away quickly rather than risk losing the line. I found that losing sight of the smaller jack in the flat game is a problem. It nestles behind the bowls in a way that completely obscures it from the mat, so you have to be prepared to go up to the head and get the exact lie of the land. If necessary, walk backwards to the mat from the head and retain a clear picture of where the jack is. Flat players instinctively know where the jack is going to flirt when they play a shot with weight. They can also assess where bowls will end up from a firing shot and this is the sort of thinking we have to gain.

That *Superbowl* triumph earned Burrows a place in the World Indoor Championships at Coatbridge, and trials for England — the first crown green specialist to receive such an honour. He reached the semi-finals at Coatbridge. He sums up bowls and looks to a number of leading crown exponents to bridge the gap over the next few years:

The flat and crown games are like badminton and tennis — similar and entirely different. Tony Poole, Allan Thompson, Mick Robinson, Gene Bardon and Robert Hitchen have all shown that they can step across from one game to the other. I look to some promising youngsters to also make their mark — such as David Holt, Neil Jenkinson and Robert Crawshaw from the North West.

The younger players are among those showing promise at the new club in Manchester, Bowlers, where Burrows is General Manager. At least an indoor club on his doorstep means that Burrows can avoid those eighty-mile round trips to Huddersfield to practise. 'I must have made ten trips over to prepare for the 1981 John Player and I played in their team and also practised at Darlington to get to know something about the game.' Burrows' fondest memory of his first year in flat bowls was a win over David Bryant in a friendly game at Darlington. As one leading bowls official said at the time: 'Bowls will never be the same again after that.' And as Burrows declared: 'The arrival of the crown green players has given a new dimension to the flat green game. Both codes can only benefit.'

NORMA SHAW

A positive approach from Norma Shaw.

Norma Shaw's bowling roots belong originally to the crown green territory of Wakefield in Yorkshire. The lady, who was to become the number one player in the women's section of flat green bowls, took her first tentative steps to the top by enjoying games of crown with husband Dennis. When they moved to Stockton, Norma's choice of house was to prove to be the turning-point in her bowling life. Norma recalls:

A cricket field backs on to the house and I remember walking round one evening. We were suddenly aware of shouts from another area and when we investigated, we found a flat bowling green. We were invited to go along and join the members in a bowl-up and it all started for me, from then. I had the good fortune to be helped by an excellent tutor in a gentleman called Herbert Wearmouth, who taught me so much about the game. Bowls is no different to any of life's lessons. If you are prepared to listen, you will learn and I got a very good grounding in the game. We would often sit watching games and Herbert would ask me which bowls I would play in certain situations. His thinking was three shots ahead and that's a policy I have tried to follow. It's advice that could benefit the many crown green ladies now trying their hand at flat. I have played against quite a few over the last couple of years, as many more are coming into our game, and I have noticed that while they have natural delivery styles, they are still learning the tactical side of the game. It's not all about getting your bowls as close as possible to the jack; it's about positional play and trying to out-think your opponent. All the possibilities need to be examined and a lot of thought given to the dangers of playing certain shots. I know from painful experience that getting a bowl too close to the jack and leaving others out of the count is dangerous. I did that against David Bryant once and he promptly fired it off. Now I realize that playing against David, you have to try to have a couple of bowls counting in case he fires. Firing is an aspect of the ladies' game that could be developed. I think we are a little worried about being embarassed, if we miss with a firing shot, so we do not try them often enough. I know that playing against David, for instance, when I have been able to outdraw him at times, he has resorted to the strike with great effect. I played him at Darlington and I used a firing shot, which I think rather surprised him. He is a nice man and a fine sportsman but I thought on that particular occasion I nearly had him in trouble. He finally won 7–5, 6–7 and 7–4, and my ambition remains to try to topple him.

Norma appeared in the first two *Superbowls* and counted some well-known bowling scalps among her haul. Using the set of bowls, which she had bought back in 1964 and never changes when playing indoors, Norma set off in the first year against the vastly experienced crown player Ken Strutt. Her control and determination on that Tuesday evening won her the game and installed Norma as a crowd favourite in a setting that, for her, was an inspiration. She won in straight sets, 7–5 and 7–3, in a game that lasted for thirteen ends and was all over in an hour. Norma's second game lasted a couple of minutes and one end longer, and was a significant victory for a lady bowler. For Norma took on the Irish giant Jim Baker, a man whose record was so impressive that many rated the former World Champion the finest indoor bowler in the game. Jim's undoing was his notorious habit of being a slow-starter and before he realized it, the popular Irishman was out of *Superbowl*. The scoreline was 7–3 and 7–6 in Norma's favour. 'It was probably my best win indoors', said Norma in a tribute to Jim Baker's considerable talents. That win gave Norma a quarter-final place against the seventeen-year-old Scottish international player, Richard Corsie. It took Norma less than an hour — forty-six minutes, in fact — and ten ends to remove young Richard. The first set lasted seven ends for a 7–3 score and it needed only three ends for a 7–1 second-set success. Ironically, forty-six minutes was the time it took Bryant to end Norma's run in the semi-final. Nine ends — five in the first and four in the second set — gave Bryant two 7–3 wins. The competition was not quite over for Norma, as the organizers of the first *Superbowl* introduced a play-off for third place. It slotted in nicely with television schedules and provided an hour and twenty-five minutes entertainment for a capacity audience in Stage One. Willie Wood, a Scottish international player for nearly twenty years, had lost to John Bell in the semi-final and was Norma's opponent for the third place position that was worth £2,000 with £1,000 for the player placed fourth. Willie was not happy with the bowls he used during his game with Bell and went back to his hotel to try his luck with another set. The new set of bowls seemed to be just the incentive Wood needed to lift his morale after losing to Bell in straight sets. He took the first set off Norma 7–2 but then crashed 7–0 in the second and the Stockton lady never allowed Wood back into the game. She wound it up with a 7–4 third-set win over a total of nineteen ends.

Reaching the semi-finals earned Norma a place in the second *Superbowl* and she started well, beating the crown green's Stan Frith in straight sets before hitting trouble in her second game. Frank McCartney, the twenty-six-year-old Scot who had won the National Indoor Singles title, ran away with the first set 7–1; Norma hit back 7–2 in the second and the scene was set for a classic finish. It failed to materialize as McCartney again stormed away for another 7–1 win and Norma's second year in *Superbowl* ended for her in the late evening on Thursday 17 October. Norma sums up her thoughts on *Superbowl*.

Reading the rink is important and I believe that is why the trial ends we are allowed can be so valuable. I firmly believe that you should find a good hand, the one that you feel comfortable on, and stick to it. Sometimes there are bad hands and they should be avoided. In *Superbowl*, the rink has developed runs that players have been anxious to avoid, switching to the other hand, if forced to. Stamina can also be an area that presents problems for ladies and I find that playing indoors can be more taxing than outdoors, where there is a spot of fresh air. It's also harder on the feet playing on the indoor rink which doesn't have the give in it that grass allows! I enjoy the sets game, although I accept that there is a line of thought that firmly believes players have a greater chance in the normal 21-up arrangement. If you are well down in a game, you do have the chance to get back and win over the 21-up game. But the sets game has worked well and provides better entertainment for viewers. You do feel that you cannot afford to make a mistake in the best-of-three-sets game and the pressure can be intense. The first end can be a little tricky for me as I feel my way but then I usually settle down. The only way to play in those conditions is to switch off completely and concentrate purely on playing. I found the *Superbowl* occasion a quite different experience to anything else I have encountered in bowls. The audience is predominantly crown green and they are not slow to encourage and cheer players on. I found it an exhilarating experience.

That experience takes its place in a career that has established Norma as the world's number one lady bowler and brought her the M.B.E. for services to bowls in the Queen's birthday honours. Norma Shaw has been bowling since 1962 and has been an England international player in every year since 1977. She has also been an outdoor international player from 1979 until her shock omission from the line-up in 1986. 'The selectors' decision to leave me out came as a shock but it will encourage me to go out and try to improve my game', is the philosophical way Norma took the incident.

TACTICS

The distinctive style of Willie Wood.

David Bryant considers the alternatives against Noel Burrows.

Tactically speaking, those of us with our bowling roots sprouting from crown green sources were in the novice class when it came to competing in the same arena as the top flat players. Their world revolves around using much heavier bowls, four instead of two, playing on flat rinks rather than undulating crown greens, and being used to matches liable to last three hours instead of the forty-five minutes or so in the crown game. So it was an education for the audience and the crown players to watch the top flat stars in action. They had learned a lot from the first competition and now they were thirsting for more tactical knowledge.

The Jeanette Conlan and David Cutler clash produced a nice line in positive thinking that won the match for the Scottish lady. At one set each and six a piece in the deciders, Cutler held shot but failed to protect his bowl. Conlan had to find a bowl of exact line and length, with almost everybody in the crowd urging her on. She kept her nerve, planted a tremendous last bowl right on the jack to lie for set and match. Cutler, with one bowl to play, was left with little option than to fire but missed and the match went to Jeanette. 'One of the greatest games of bowls you will ever see', summed up commentator, Hugh Johns. That was a head that was crucial to either player, yet there was nothing in the build-up that made allowances for the use of bowls beyond the jack and nothing in the way of masking shots in the front.

By the time Jeanette played Jim Baker in her next game, there was an opportunity to study the defensive qualities. Jeanette had won the first set 7–3 and they were tied at 5–5 in the second. The shot was held by Jeanette, with a bowl played on the forehand which settled at 11 o' clock (on the clock face used to describe the appearance of heads). The danger was that if Conlan's bowl was played on to with some weight, the jack would be sprung free towards the back of the head. She realized the danger and played her last bowl to a five o' clock position, diagonally across from her shot bowl. This insurance policy paid handsome dividends as she forced Baker into a firing shot which missed. Had contact been made, Jeanette had taken the necessary precaution to still have the angle in her favour to count.

Tactics were evident again when Jeanette played her last game in *Superbowl* 1985 against the shrewdest brain in the game — David Bryant. The master had tested Jeanette with a mixture of jack lengths and use of the mat. He won the first set and at 6–2 in the second had taken the shot with a toucher. Again, the weakness was that Bryant had left the bowl exposed and invitingly available to be played out. He inspected the head and opted to go for a positional bowl on the backhand which came to rest ideally, in the five o' clock area. Contact on the shot bowl would release the jack and squirt it towards Bryant's back 'insurance' bowl. Conlan went for it on the backhand, took out the shot bowl but Bryant's second was still close enough to count for the game. This tactical awareness and ability to take decisions, once made, were qualities that the World Champion describes as, 'True grit. She will be the next Norma Shaw.'

Noel Burrows versus Willie Wood in the semi-final saw tactics of the highest quality constantly in use. Both players had been careful to select strong bowls to counter a notorious run in the rink that had worried other players. Wood took the first set and Burrows the second, by a staggering 7–1 margin. Burrows led 4–3 in the third set and played a bowl that dropped 45.5 cm (18 in) short on the forehand. Wood's reply, on the forehand, came through and allowed Burrows again to exploit the forehand route in the drawing line which was cut off to Wood, who had to switch to the backhand approach that was unpopular. His bowl fell short and well out of the count being about 2 metres (2 yards) adrift. But Burrows was now able to use Wood's first bowl behind the jack as a drawing target on the backhand, not wishing to disturb anything on the other hand. This time his bowl held up as it seemed to hit the run in the rink and it stayed out. The importance of Wood's back bowl then came into the picture as the Scot played his final bowl on the backhand. It avoided bowls in the approach to the head and rested neatly on his own back bowl to take the end. The lessons highlighted were the importance of a back bowl and the problems in changing the hand, which means changing the weight of delivery. It is a test of the bowler's ability to read the weight of the green, which can differ on each hand.

The situation after that end was that both players were left with three to win the match and the obvious danger was that the game could be settled at a single end. Neither player had scored more than two at any previous end in their game, so the odds were against it. Wood elected to go on the forehand with his lead and was 15 cm (6 in) short. Burrows found the same line with a bowl 23 cm (9 in) short and good enough to prevent Wood getting a big score at that end. Switching to the backhand, Burrows was left with a choice of either hand, as the split just in front of the jack had left his first bowl in the forehand draw and Wood's shot bowl on the backhand. He gave his bowl extra weight and ran off his own front bowl to play out Wood's; he then clipped the jack nicely to lie with two. Wood tried the backhand and found a good line but appeared to be too short to be in the count. His sad expression as he studied the head told all. Burrows was unable to make it three for the game but he left his last bowl in the drawing line and forced Wood to change his hand. Wood took a wider course and his bowl responded sufficiently to encourage the marker to indicate that he felt Burrows had only one shot counting with a measure for second. Burrows decided to take a look for himself. The decision he took after inspecting the head was crucial. He went for the kill on the forehand to make a certain count with his last wood. It was a certain two and a measure; and, after a couple of checks, the game was given to Burrows. Burrows then had the triple count he needed to win the match and he revealed to me later that he was convinced he was already in with a double, to which he had to add one for game. The opinion of the marker at such an important stage of the game was that it was worth a measure and that was fair enough. But the lesson from Burrows was that it is worth examining the head, looking at the lie of the land from all directions and, if you are confident in your own mind, then you must have the courage of your convictions and go for the percentage shot — a winner.

Tactics may be enthralling but without sportsmanship, *Superbowl* would never enjoy that special rapport that exists between players and spectators. This was never more apparent than in the classic final between Burrows and Bryant. Burrows had taken two sets, Bryant one and the scores were level at 6–6 in the fourth of the five-set game. Bryant set the mark, ran 1 metre (1 yard) through with his lead. Burrows, on the same forehand, was better and counted with a bowl 15 cm (6 in) short of being jack high. Bryant, still forehand, ran into the back of Burrows' shot wood, slightly opening the head. Burrows stayed on the forehand, trying to block the route in again, but his bowl cut across the head into the backhand draw, leaving a firing target. Bryant went through again, on the forehand, to have two bowls behind the jack but not counting. Burrows tried the backhand and touched the jack to lie with two, although one was enough to win the match. Now Bryant had several options — he could play the jack into a ditch, for instance. In the event, he played a firing shot, clipped one of Burrows' bowls but still appeared to leave one in, that would have cost him the game. Bryant walked the length of the rink, had one brief look at the head and quickly offered a match-conceding handshake. Burrows won the match while Bryant won the hearts of a capacity crowd with his sporting reaction to what must have been a bitter blow to his pride. It was a gesture by the man whom all, including Burrows, readily acknowledged was still 'the world's number one'.

THE FUTURE

Tony Allcock (right) in his role as a commentator. He is pictured here with presenter, Elton Welsby.

What does the future hold for *Superbowl* after its instant success as a competition to rank alongside the best in bowls? The original concept of pitting the top flat and crown players against each other was realized when Noel Burrows beat David Bryant in the second year. The success of the women players, particularly Norma Shaw and Jeanette Conlan, justified their inclusion, despite original misgivings by some bowling officials. There is no doubt that the indoor game with the focus on one rink is tailor-made for television, lending itself to overhead shots for the tacticians among viewers and the ability to transmit the live reaction of the audience inside the arena.

Superbowl went into areas of bowls that traditionalists tried to resist. The sets game and the decision to attach microphones to umpires were developments that raised eyebrows. This last move was regarded by some as an intrusion into an area that was strictly the preserve of players and officials on the rink, at least that was the thinking before *Superbowl* burst on to the scene. Granada's Head of Sport, Paul Doherty says:

> We have tried to put flesh on the bones. Sport has never been projected in this way; we put the emphasis on the people and their characters; we used new ideas and looked not just at bowling but at entertainment. We are investing a great deal of money in developing bowls into a major sport. There are people in bowls whose interest is in making a quick kill, but this does not apply to the television companies. We are not in bowls to be governed by antiquated thinking. The traditionalists are in danger of killing the game. Their thinking on allowing women to take part, on the three sets and on the 'miking' of umpires was typical.

The Liverpool Victoria Insurance Company, who took a considerable financial interest in the event, saw *Superbowl* as the ideal vehicle to promote their name on a national basis. Sponsorship has been taking an increasing stake in bowls—flat and crown—and helps take some of the financial burden off organizers. 'The decision to sponsor *Superbowl* was taken in a week', reveals Brian Low, Marketing Manager of Liverpool Victoria Insurance Company. 'Three weeks after the initial approach from Granada, Liverpool Victoria's name was emblazoned on our television screens.' 'A sponsorship scoop', was how Ken Wilkinson, Liverpool Victoria's Chairman described his company's involvement.

On the playing side, Doherty looks forward to the crown green players shedding what appeared to be something of an inferiority complex in the early days of *Superbowl*. He believes that the difference in skill between the two codes will disappear in a few years. Then Granada will have to take a fresh look at *Superbowl*. Crown green bowls has taken the hint and thousands of players in the north-west of England have taken up the flat challenge. Out of *Superbowl* have come flat green indoor centres at Blackpool, Oldham, Swinton (near Manchester) and in the industrial estate of Trafford Park, where Noel Burrows and a group of business friends have opened the world's biggest indoor bowls centre, with fourteen rinks.

'*Superbowl* has made great television entertainment', sums up Doherty. Subject to the increased involvement of I.T.V., and with time and full co-operation, the present tournament might lead, in the future, to such events as a World Superbowl or, looking to the game's long-term future even a Junior Superbowl.

SUPERBOWL

First Round

GORDON NIVEN (F) beat Stan Frith (C) 5–7, 7–6, 7–2
ROY WHITE (F) beat Vernon Lee (C) 7–5, 7–4
WILLIE WOOD (F) beat Mal Hughes (F) 6–7, 7–2, 7–2
BOB SUTHERLAND (F) beat Mike Robinson (C) 7–6, 7–3
JOHN BELL (F) beat Brian Duncan (C) 7–5, 3–7, 7–3
DAVIE GOURLAY (F) beat Harold Barlow (C) 7–2, 7–1
NOEL BURROWS (C) beat Michael Dunlop (F) 7–6, 7–3
KAREN GALVIN (C) beat Jean Vallis (F) 7–5, 7–4
NORMA SHAW (F) beat Ken Strutt (C) 7–5, 7–3
JIM BAKER (F) beat Len Higginbottom (C) 4–7, 7–2, 7–2
ROBERT HITCHEN (C) beat Steve Nixon (C) 6–7, 7–3, 7–3
RICHARD CORSIE (F) beat Michael Leach (C) 7–1, 7–2
NIGEL SMITH (F) beat Norman Fletcher (C) 7–1, 7–5
SARAH GOURLAY (F) beat Freda Locke (C) 7–1, 7–5
RAY HILL (F) beat Christine Knowles (C) 7–3, 7–0
DAVID BRYANT (F) beat Arthur Murray (C) 7–0, 7–2

Second Round

GORDON NIVEN (F) beat Roy White (F) 7–6, 3–7, 7–3
WILLIE WOOD (F) beat Bob Sutherland (F) 7–2, 7–3
JOHN BELL (F) beat Davie Gourlay (F) 7–4, 7–0
NOEL BURROWS (C) beat Karen Galvin (C) 7–5, 7–0
NORMA SHAW (F) beat Jim Baker (F) 7–3, 7–6
RICHARD CORSIE (F) beat Robert Hitchen (C) 7–0, 7–4
NIGEL SMITH (F) beat Sarah Gourlay (F) 7–1, 7–5
DAVID BRYANT (F) beat Ray Hill (F) 7–6, 7–3

Quarter Finals

WILLIE WOOD (F) beat Gordon Niven (F) 7–3, 7–4
JOHN BELL (F) beat Noel Burrows (C) 7–4, 4–7, 7–3
NORMA SHAW (F) beat Richard Corsie (F) 7–3, 7–1
DAVID BRYANT (F) beat Nigel Smith (F) 7–3, 6–7, 7–5

Semi Finals

JOHN BELL (F) beat Willie Wood (F) 7–2, 7–5
DAVID BRYANT (F) beat Norma Shaw (F) 7–3, 7–3

RESULTS 1984

Third/fourth Place Play-off

NORMA SHAW (F) beat Willie Wood (F) 2–7, 7–0, 7–4

Final

DAVID BRYANT (F) beat John Bell (F) 5–7, 7–6, 7–6

1984 Superbowl Champion

DAVID BRYANT, C.B.E.

David Bryant, three times World Champion and winner of Superbowl *1984, defending his* Superbowl *title in 1985.*

SUPERBOWL *(Sponsored by Liverpool Victoria Insurance)*

First Round

JIM BOYLE (F) beat Nancy Gibson (F) 7–1, 7–2
TONY ALLCOCK (F) beat Robert Hitchen (C) 7–2, 7–1
NORMAN FLETCHER (C) beat Andy Ross (F) 7–4, 2–7, 7–2
DAVID BRYANT (F) beat Mick Robinson (C) 7–6, 7–4
JIM BAKER (F) beat Vernon Lee (C) 7–5, 7–2
RICHARD BRITTAN (C) beat Allan Thompson (C) 7–2, 0–7, 7–3
DAVID CUTLER (F) beat Arthur Murray (C) 7–0, 7–2
JEANETTE CONLAN (F) beat Len Higginbottom (C) 7–4, 2–7, 7–6
SYLVIA JONES (C) beat Diane Priestley (C) 6–7, 7–5, 7–3
TONY POOLE (C) beat Terry Sullivan (F) 7–6, 7–2
JOHN BELL (F) beat Christine Knowles (C) 2–7, 7–3, 7–1
WILLIE WOOD (F) beat Peter Evans (F) 7–2, 7–2
JULIE DAVIES (F) beat Karen Galvin (C) 7–1, 7–5
NOEL BURROWS (C) beat Rodney McCutcheon (F) 7–3, 6–7, 7–1
NORMA SHAW (F) beat Stan Frith (C) 7–1, 7–3
FRANK McCARTNEY (F) beat Brian Duncan (C) 7–4, 3–7, 7–5

Second Round

JIM BOYLE (F) beat Tony Allcock (F) 2–7, 7–2, 7–4
DAVID BRYANT (F) beat Norman Fletcher (C) 7–0, 5–7, 7–5
JIM BAKER (F) beat Richard Brittan (C) 7–2, 7–5
JEANETTE CONLAN (F) beat David Cutler (F) 6–7, 7–5, 7–6
TONY POOLE (C) beat Sylvia Jones (C) 7–1, 7–0
WILLIE WOOD (F) beat John Bell (F) 7–4, 7–2
NOEL BURROWS (C) beat Julie Davies (F) 6–7, 7–3, 7–6
FRANK McCARTNEY (F) beat Norma Shaw (F) 7–1, 2–7, 7–1

Quarter Finals

DAVID BRYANT (F) beat Jim Boyle (F) 7–2, 7–2
JEANETTE CONLAN (F) beat Jim Baker (F) 7–3, 7–5
WILLIE WOOD (F) beat Tony Poole (C) 7–1, 7–4
NOEL BURROWS (C) beat Frank McCartney (F) 7–1, 2–7, 7–1

Semi Finals

DAVID BRYANT (F) beat Jeanette Conlan (F) 7–0, 7–2
NOEL BURROWS (C) beat Willie Wood (F) 5–7, 7–1, 7–4

RESULTS 1985

Final

NOEL BURROWS (C) beat David Bryant (F) 7–6, 7–5, 0–7, 7–6

1985 Liverpool Victoria Insurance Superbowl Champion
NOEL BURROWS

Noel Burrows, Superbowl *Champion 1985.*

SUPERBOWL

Play in *Superbowl* is in accordance with the official set of rules laid down by the British Isles Indoor Bowls Council, but there are certain areas which are brought to the attention of officials and players before play starts. Competitors are advised about their mode of dress before they arrive at Stage One, and they are provided with a red and a blue sports shirt. Flat green men players are asked to wear white slacks and crown green men grey. The ladies, too, get a red shirt and a blue shirt each and they are required to wear the regulation grey skirt. The brief given to players before play starts also includes a timely reminder to crown green players that they must wear the appropriate soft, flat shoes to avoid damaging the carpet. This practice has long been established in the flat game and it is becoming standard, as the gospel is spread throughout the crown green world. *Superbowl's* lead on footwear has been taken up by the British Crown Green Association who now warn players in their official handbook: leather, hard or block-heeled footwear should not be worn whilst on the green. This instruction refers to their outdoor game. Advertising a company's goods is another area that gets special attention in the pre-competition briefing. No sponsorship name, other than the manufacturer's logo, is permitted on any item of clothing. This is laid down under the Indoor Bowling Association regulations.

The following brief is issued before the competition begins:

Toss of coin

Before appearing on the green, the umpire will arrange for the toss of a coin between players. The winner of the toss has the choice of either taking the mat and jack, or giving it to his opponent before the first and third sets. The loser of the toss has the choice before the start of the second set.

Trial ends

As in many major bowling tournaments, there will be two trial ends, of *two* bowls each, before every match except the final. Before the final, each player will be allowed *four* bowls on each of the two trial ends.

Placing mat on first end

Law 24, which indicates that the back end of the mat must be 1.2 metres (4 ft) from the ditch applies only to the first end of the first set. It does not apply to the first end of the second or third sets.

Minimum mat distance on all ends

A small 'T' will be chalked 2 metres (6 ft) from the ditch at each end of the green to assist players when they wish to place the mat the minimum 2 metres (6 ft) between the front end and the ditch. [It will also assist markers in placing the jack when the jack is delivered to a point less than 2 metres (6 ft) from the ditch.]

RULES OF PLAY

No running on green

Both crown green and level green bowlers run on outdoor greens. Every indoor club prohibits running on indoor carpets because of possible damage to, or disturbance of, the carpet, both of which affect the running of the bowl. It is for this reason, and not specifically because the portable rink being used is in 2.4 metres x 1.2 metres (8 ft x 4 ft) sections under the carpet, that no running will be permitted on the green. Umpires will understand that there will be a natural inclination to run, through sheer enthusiasm. They will, however, be looking out for deliberate repetition of this offence. It is in the interests of all competitors that no player, official, or any other person should run on the bowling surface.

Measuring by umpire

If either player requires measurement for shot at the conclusion of an end, in accordance with the convention established at recent major events, this will be done by neither player nor marker. The first and only measuring will be done by the umpire, who will signal his decision by turning out the winning bowl.

Possession of rink

Law 50 indicates that possession of the rink passes to the other player when the bowl comes to rest. It is not possible for a player to walk up the rink and be behind the jack when the bowl comes to rest. The only way of ensuring Law 50 is observed is to be behind the mat when the bowl comes to rest.

Foot-faulting

Because of the difference between a crown green footer and a level green mat, there are significant differences between the laws of foot-faulting in the two codes. Crown green law 4 requires contact between toe and footer, while the corresponding law 27 requires one foot to be entirely within the confines of the mat, either on or above the mat. During the practice sessions the umpires will keep a friendly eye on delivery actions and advise accordingly.

Indication of shot

The World Indoor Bowls Council and the British Isles Indoor Bowls Council have recently indicated their approval of efforts to keep 'live spectators' advised as to which bowler is holding shot, and how many shots there are during the progress of an end. The method of doing this, using the 'lollipop signals', will be demonstrated during the practice sessions, for markers to use during the *Superbowl*. It will be done in a way which prevents the bowler being distracted by movement while he or she is on the mat. As with any other indication of opinion by the marker on the subject — if it is important to the bowler to *know* who is holding shot, he is advised to determine his own view.

GLOSSARY

Bowls has a language of its own and expressions can vary in the flat and crown versions. Here is a selection of the better-known terms in common use throughout the world of bowls.

Flat Green

Back bowl	Bowl that comes to rest behind the head — often used when an opponent might try to move the jack.
Backhand	Bowl delivered with the bias against the thumb of a right-handed player and aimed towards its target on the left of the centre line.
Bank	Outer wall of the ditch around the green and above the playing level.
Burnt end	Term used in the U.S.A. and Canada to describe a dead end.
Dead bowl	A bowl which rests outside the boundaries of the rink and has not touched the jack; or a bowl which is played out by another bowl.
Dead draw	A wood which settles exactly where required.
Dead end	When the jack is played outside the boundary. The end can be replayed from where it started.
Ditches	Channels around the green normally filled with pebbles.
Draw	The direction the bowl takes in its approach to the jack.
Fire	A powerful delivery designed to remove the jack or bowls. Also called drive or strike.
Forehand	The bias held against the little finger of a right-handed player. Aimed at the right side of the rink.
Heavy	A bowl played with too much weight which finishes well past the point at which it is aimed.
Jack	Round, white ball, sometimes called the kitty, at which the bowls are aimed. In flat it has no bias, but in crown it has.
Jack high	A bowl that settles with its front level with the front of the jack.
Mat	Rectangular strip of rubber measuring 61 cm x 35.5 cm (24 in x 14 in).
Measure	When there is any doubt about which bowls are nearest the jack, a measure is used to determine an end. No measuring can take place until an end is complete.
Open the end	Firing shot that clears away bowls around the jack.
Rest	A bowl played to come to rest on another.
Rink	The playing area.
Rub	A bowl which glances off another and has its course altered.

Shot	The bowl lying nearest to the jack, and in a winning position.
Showing eyes	A bowl that wobbles along and shows the white discs clearly. The discs are known as the eyes of the bowl.
Spring	When the jack is forced back and rebounds off a bowl to spring free.
Toucher	A bowl that touches the jack during its run and remains within the playing area of the rink. It can also stay live if it is in the ditch. A toucher is marked in chalk.
Trail	A bowl that connects with the jack and carries it a short distance.
Trial ends	Two practice ends before the start of play to give players a feel of the rink.
Weight	The force which needs to be applied in delivering a bowl; it is determined by the pace of the green.
Wick	A bowl that strikes another on the side and has its course altered. Also referred to as a chip, slither or jive.
Yard through	A bowl that is played with extra weight to travel a yard past the jack.

Crown Green

Block	Also known as the jack (see jack, Flat Green).
Bobby	A bowl played to bar the approach to the jack.
Cut	Ditch around the green.
Dead end	Void end
Dead wood	One that cannot score because of rule-breaking.
End	Starts with the bowling of the jack and finishes with the arrival of the last bowl.
Enid Blyton	A short (story) mark.
Falling mark	Where the slope of the green makes the bowls fall against the bias.
Feet	Traditional cry to warn players to avoid approaching bowls.
Finger peg	Jack or bowl delivered with the bias against the little finger.
Fire	A shot delivered with force to remove another bowl or the jack (also known as strike).
Heavy going	Slow-running green.
Jack header	A wood that finishes in front and touches the jack.
Length	Delivering a bowl of perfect strength.
Mark	When the jack is delivered the correct minimum distance of 19 metres (17 yards).

Mat	Round and made of rubber. Players must place toe on mat — also known as the footer — when delivering the jack or a bowl. The mat must have a diameter of not less than 12.5 cm (5 in) and not more than 15 cm (6 in).
Narrow	A bowl that is delivered too far inside the line of the jack.
Peg	Also called the bias of the jack or bowl.
Round peg	When the jack or bowls are sent on their way with the bias away from the crown of the green.
Straight peg	The jack or bowls delivered with the bias facing the crown and balancing out the natural fall of the land.
Strike-out	Time at which players who have not arrived are scratched out of a competition.
Tapes	Another word for measures.
Through	A bowl that is played with additional strength and runs through the end.
Thumb peg	When the bias of the jack or bowl is held against the thumb of a right-handed player.
Wobbled	A jack or bowl delivered badly; it bounces out of the hand.
Wood	Strictly used to describe a bowl made from lignum vitae and not one of the composition variety.